Cloud Capacity Management

Navin Sabharwal

Prashant Wali

Cloud Capacity Management

ISBN-13 (pbk): 978-1-4302-4923-8

ISBN-13 (electronic): 978-1-4302-4924-5

President and Publisher: Paul Manning
Lead Editor: Saswata Mishra
Editorial Board: Steve Anglin, Ewan Buckingham, Gary Cornell, Louise Corrigan, Morgan Ertel, Jonathan Gennick, Jonathan Hassell, Robert Hutchinson, Michelle Lowman, James Markham, Matthew Moodie, Jeff Olson, Jeffrey Pepper, Douglas Pundick, Ben Renow-Clarke, Dominic Shakeshaft, Gwenan Spearing, Steve Weiss, Tom Welsh
Coordinating Editor: Jill Balzano
Copy Editors: Mary Behr
Compositor: SPi Global
Indexer: SPi Global
Artist: SPi Global
Cover Designer: Anna Ishchenko

Distributed to the book trade worldwide by Springer Science+Business Media New York, 233 Spring Street, 6th Floor, New York, NY 10013. Phone 1-800-SPRINGER, fax (201) 348-4505, e-mail orders-ny@springer-sbm.com, or visit www.springeronline.com.

For information on translations, please e-mail rights@apress.com, or visit www.apress.com.

Apress and friends of ED books may be purchased in bulk for academic, corporate, or promotional use. eBook versions and licenses are also available for most titles. For more information, reference our Special Bulk Sales–eBook Licensing web page at www.apress.com/bulk-sales.

Any source code or other supplementary materials referenced by the author in this text is available to readers at www.apress.com. For detailed information about how to locate your book's source code, go to www.apress.com/source-code.

Dedicated to my lovely family and my deity, Lord Shiva.

— Prashant Wali

Dedicated to the people I love and the God I trust.

— Navin Sabharwal

Contents at a Glance

Contents

About the Authors

Navin Sabharwal is an innovator, thought leader, author, and consultant in the areas of IT service management, product development, intellectual property creation, cloud computing, cloud lifecycle management, and software product development.

Navin has created niche award-winning products and solutions and has filed numerous patents in diverse fields such as IT services, assessment engines, ranking algorithms, capacity planning engines, and knowledge management.

Navin leads the automation and cloud computing practice for HCL Technologies' Infrastructure Services Division. Navin holds a Masters in Information Technology and is a Certified Project Management Professional.

Prashant Wali is working with a leading Indian multinational IT company as a consultant and holds a B.Tech/MBA in IT from Symbiosis International University in India. He is currently handling multiple cloud service areas like product management, technology incubation, pre-sales, and ITSM process consulting.

He has extensive experience in all facets of infrastructure management combined with process, tool, and development experience in cloud computing and IT infrastructure management. His areas of expertise include product and IP creation in the cloud domain, product engineering, cloud/ITSM consulting, capacity management, infrastructure monitoring, tool automation, ITILv3 process design, implementation, and statistics.

Acknowledgments

Special thanks go out to Anant Gupta, R. Srikrishna, C.R.D. Prasad, C. Vijay Kumar, and Kalyan Kumar for all the inspiration and support. Also, this book would not have been possible without Saswata Mishra and the rest of the team at Apress. It has been wonderful to work with the Apress team.

Preface

There has been hype about cloud computing for years. It's often makes headlines in IT news. Why not? Cloud computing has revolutionized the entire backbone of computing technology and is helping organizations in aligning IT with business needs. Cloud computing is most definitely part of the future of IT services as it enables businesses to focus more on profit making without worrying too much about business enablers like hardware. Cloud computing, in short, ensures optimum capacity utilization of IT resources in a cost-effective fashion.

The cloud computing concepts and availability of IT resources on demand have a drastic impact on the way capacity planning is executed. This book covers capacity management principles and practices as applied to cloud service models in private and public clouds.

Conventional capacity management processes need to be adapted in a cloud environment. Procedures to carry out capacity management may remain the same, but activities and techniques constituting existing procedures certainly will change in a cloud environment. The prime motivation to write this book is to help readers understand and apply new capacity management procedures and techniques to fulfill infrastructure demand for supporting business processes and applications.

The cloud computing wave is changing the way organizations consume information technology. The shift to cloud computing and virtualization is posing new challenges in implementing the traditional ITIL processes in a dynamic environment.

IT managers will want to implement traditional capacity management best practices for adoption in cloud computing environments wherein multiple stakeholders, high levels of abstraction, consolidation, virtualization of IT infrastructure, dynamic cost models, etc. are involved. This book takes a pragmatic approach to implementing best practices for capacity management and virtualization techniques that will help cloud service providers in designing and implementing capacity management processes in the most cost-effective fashion.

This book gives significant emphasis to cloud service models and the value chain in which capacity management and planning have different implications for various stakeholders like cloud service creators, cloud service aggregators, and cloud service consumers. Thus, this book intends to take the audience from the basics of cloud computing and virtualization to understanding various models of cloud computing—and how to change and implement the capacity planning processes while keeping in mind the new model.

This book covers the capacity management process in two parts. The first part focuses on capacity planning for new services, and the second part covers performance monitoring or capacity management for ongoing services in a cloud environment. Businesses running on deployment models like the cloud must be able to cope with demand spikes so that cost-effective infrastructure capacity is provided over time to support business operations and to ensure business continuity and desired business results. After reading this book we hope that you will come away with a clear understanding of the potential usefulness of the cloud and models that might make sense for you in your efforts to cost effectively manage your capacity needs.

Introduction

We started writing this book in 2011. As a part of a cloud solution and product development team, we came across repetitive questions while building cloud solutions. How will capacity be planned and managed by cloud providers? Is infinite capacity possible? We also witnessed chaotic discussions and fierce debates on how service providers will manage resource capacity in a cloud environment at all levels, be it business, service, or component. Is it really possible to have infinite capacity in a cloud environment, and if yes, then how? Every time these basic questions popped up, everybody had an opinion—but no two were the same. We started with our introspection and attempted to answer those questions considering ourselves as service providers. In fact, while writing this, two of our team members were talking about cloud scalability and designed a solution around it for an RFP response. Lunch conversations at the company café with server automation and solution architects, statisticians, process consultants, service owners gave rise to diverse views whenever cloud capacity and scalability were discussed.

Since the beginning, cloud computing has created gigabytes of questions in everyone's mind, be it technology guys or business people. At the very least people were fascinated by the name. So let's start with a basic definition: cloud computing refers to the usage and access of computer resources over the Internet or a digital network. Technology and business people we encounter everyday are clueless about the workings and techniques behind private and public cloud capacity management, and there is a lot of white space in this area. Capacity management is and will continue to be the basis for the lion's share of benefits and praise bestowed upon the art of cloud computing presently.

All companies providing cloud infrastructure services have to seek an approach on the basis of which they can without any hesitation offer optimized solutions. This is not an area where the suppliers are saying "no." Resource utilization and planning for capacity are the key areas that sit at the heart of cloud capacity management.

Capacity needs, associated with a service, must be addressed at all layers (i.e., business capacity, service capacity, and resource/component capacity). It's important to have a clear understanding of how these layers are dependent on each other from top to bottom and how these behave when there are changes in service demand, service levels, and other business process changes.

There are various types of clouds: public cloud, community cloud, private cloud, etc. The latest analyst reports suggest that the cloud market will continue to grow exponentially. Worldwide companies are investing in cloud services or strategically intend to do so in coming years.

This book primarily deals with capacity planning for enterprises interested in setting up a private cloud. Capacity management procedures must address capacity-related needs for both new services and ongoing services. Capacity management for new services must seek inputs from demand data to determine capacity requirements in terms of datacenter space, resource, and performance requirements (i.e., network, storage, compute, etc.); service levels also must be known in order to set up performance benchmarks. If disaster recovery requirements are necessary, capacity has to be tuned accordingly. Similar tuning has to be done to handle seasonality and other demand regulatory measures that are required by the demand management process. On the basis of capacity needs, capacity design and planning are required to take care of all capacity-related needs for running the business.

In contrast, capacity management for current services is primarily an iterative process of regulating and tuning capacity along with performance monitoring. Monitoring tools play a major role here in order to keep an eye on resource usage and other performance-related meters.

What This Book Offers

This book first helps readers understand what cloud computing is and the stakeholders involved in delivering value in the cloud value chain. Cloud service delivery is explained through service- and layer-based views of the cloud. Capacity management processes are explained to help readers understand their relevance and importance in delivering IT services in a cloud computing environment. Then capacity management is explained in business, service, and component terms. This book will also help readers understand what capacity management means for the cloud service creator, cloud service aggregator, and the cloud service consumer.

As we know, the cloud environment includes a high level of abstraction and virtualization to facilitate rapid and on-demand provisioning of services in a pay-as-you-go cost model. This differs from conventional IT service models, which utilize a traditional approach when planning for service capacity in order to provide optimum services levels.

This book offers a helpful blend of IT service management (ITSM) best practices and on-the-ground technical implementation of these practices in the various cloud scenarios for infrastructure capacity planning and optimization activities. The book also educates readers concerning an integrated scenario of how ITSM best practices for capacity planning get addressed in the cloud environment.

It also addresses cloud computing basics, cloud computing models, the impact of cloud computing on capacity planning, traditional versus cloud capacity, and capacity management process implementations in cloud environments showcasing toolset capabilities and techniques for capacity planning and performance management. Capacity management from the cloud service provider's view has been segregated into capacity management for new services and ongoing capacity management of live services.

- Procedures are explained for capacity planning of new services to ensure cost-justifiable capacity. These include procedures like understanding capacity requirements, documenting and designing capacity techniques, and producing a capacity plan for new services.

- For live services, techniques for infrastructure performance monitoring and optimization are explained to ensure that agreed upon performance levels and appropriate capacity is provided. These include procedures like implementing capacity design, analysis, tuning, and capacity monitoring.

Tools and techniques are explained to ensure implementation of

- Best practices for capacity planning.
- Best practices for ongoing performance monitoring.

Techniques like dynamic resource scheduling, scaling, load balancing, and clustering are explained for implementing capacity management; these are aligned with capacity management procedures using best practices.

This book also covers emerging techniques in capacity management like self learning systems, yield management, and proactive capacity planning to make readers aware of the latest in the capacity management area. Additionally, emphasis is given on how capacity models like business capacity, service capacity, and component capacity are collectively influenced by service demand, varying performance needs, and SLAs.

Before moving ahead, it's important to understand how a cloud service delivery model is formed. Chapter 1 defines cloud computing and the various deployment models.

■ ■ ■

Understanding Cloud Computing

This chapter covers the basic concepts of cloud computing, cloud technology, and its ingredients. Before diving deeply into capacity management, it's important to have a clear understanding of the technology definitions. Cloud computing characteristics, deployment, and service models have been simplified in order to set the context for subsequent chapters. Besides cloud basics, this chapter discusses the impact of cloud computing on enterprises. This chapter also makes readers understand how the role of enterprise IT changes when cloud solutions are considered. Under the purview of cloud computing, the traditional IT landscape seeks transformation in order to support business applications efficiently and effectively.

Cloud Computing

Cloud computing is a buzzword these days. CIOs and key decision makers are seriously considering aligning IT with the cloud—the same cloud many of them discarded as a worthless idea in the year 2008. It is predicted that CIOs will continue to increase investments in cloud computing.

In Gartner's latest quarterly IT spending report, the research firm for the first time broke out cloud computing as a separate forecast category, providing an in-depth analysis of current and future cloud spending trends. The hottest growth in the cloud market in the coming year will be in Infrastructure as a Service (IaaS), which is expected to grow by 41%. Management and security is the second-hottest cloud growth area, expected to rise 27.2%, with platform as a service (26.6%), SaaS (17.4%), and business process as a service (15%) rounding out the top five. "The cloud market is growing at a pretty rapid clip," Anderson says. "Cloud services within the broader IT spending market are still small, but the growth rate looks promising."

Source: Gartner Quarterly IT spending Report 2012.

All technology providers are publicizing their cloud computing capabilities, or at least their strategies for the cloud. Cloud computing hype is inundating the IT world like no other hype before. In fact, the impact of cloud computing has been realized way beyond the critical interpretations.

Virtualization technology, which is at the heart of cloud computing, appeared magically, right on cue, when it could be put to excellent use for optimized data center operations. *Revolution* is the word that truly interprets the impact of cloud computing on the way technology is being offered.

As defined by the National Institute of Technology and Standards, cloud computing is a model for enabling convenient, on-demand network access to a shared pool of configurable computing resources (such as networks, servers, storage, applications, and services) that can be rapidly provisioned and released with minimal management effort or service provider interaction. Such a cloud model promotes availability and is composed of five essential characteristics, three service models, and four deployment models.

The primary benefit of cloud computing solutions is a lower total cost of ownership (TCO) that results from the more efficient utilization of resources through resource pooling and the leveraging of technology. For example, through the use of virtualization technology, several servers may be consolidated into just one physical server, resulting in reduced cost and enhanced support capabilities via centralized services management. Figure 1-1 depicts a conventional on-premises IT model of a typical enterprise with the IT back bone supporting enterprise functions at all levels (i.e., back office, middle office, and front office).

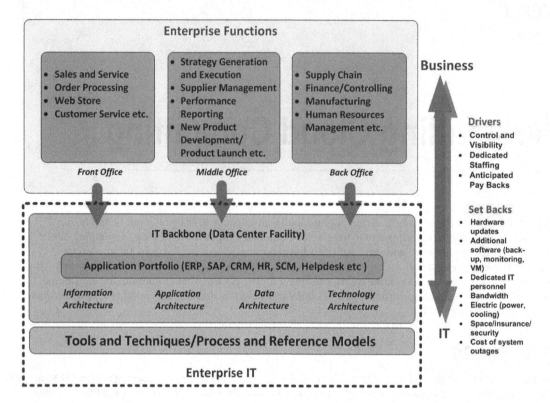

Figure 1-1. On-premise enterprise IT

On-premise IT, if compared with cloud-based IT, generally takes the back seat considering factors like cost, functionality, speed of deployment. Moreover, possibility of errors by IT personnel and lack of standardization have historically caused more worries to CIOs than with large cloud providers today.

With the new age of cloud computing, IT is providing business agility, resilience, and profits to the enterprise.

Cloud Characteristics

There are several variations of the cloud definition and the characteristics associated with cloud computing. We will cover the basics and make it easy for the readers of this book to understand the essential characteristics and why they are important.

On-Demand Availability of Services

This characteristic is essential in a cloud service In traditional IT environments, there is no on-demand availability of services; typically one has to go through a long procurement process to get an application or an IT service. As an example of Infrastructure as a Service (Iaas), the cloud provides compute, network, storage, and security services on demand. As a result, users that require infrastructure services can order them and get them at the click of a button, rather than wait for a lengthy procurement process to complete before the capacity of a particular service is delivered. In other words, cloud providers have systems that can provide compute and other resources on demand to the users without any hassles.

Standardization and automation in a cloud computing environment enable agility and on-demand provisioning of resources. In fact, one can use a credit card to purchase compute capacity and have a virtual instance running in the cloud in a matter of minutes. Thus, cloud computing enables immediate access to resources when demanded by the users or applications.

Network Access

The cloud services are available on the Internet and can be accessed through multiple modes of connectivity including dedicated connections. The connectivity is based on open standards. Thus, cloud computing—just like the Internet—crosses national boundaries and provides services to the world.

Pooling of Resources

The cloud provider creates a pool of compute capacity that is offered to multiple customers or tenants. The cloud provider makes an upfront investment in creating a cloud service and has ready capacity to offer to customers.

The pooled resources allow multiple customers to leverage the service and use the shared infrastructure for their requirements. The consumer may not have exact knowledge of the location of the service being offered, though they may choose the continent, country, or approximate location from where services are offered. The cloud provider has automations and dynamic placement engines in place that ensure that the capacity is shared across customers and that they get sufficient resources to run their applications.

The cloud provider thus acts as an owner of the cloud computing resources that are rented out to multiple customers, who use it in a shared model. The concept is similar to the way a taxi or a bus service works, wherein a bus or taxi is used by multiple tenants but it is owned by someone else.

The cloud provider ensures security and confidentiality of customer information and has systems in place to ensure one customer's resources or data is not accessed by the other customers hosted on the same physical resources. Thus, network bandwidth, compute cycles, memory, and storage are resources in IaaS that are offered as a shared pool of resources to customers.

Elasticity

The cloud provider builds the service with scalability in mind. As a result, all aspects of the cloud service should be elastic and scalable.

As the usage of an application grows, the customers can order more capacity from the cloud provider in an automated fashion. Applications that require a rapid scale up or down in capacity are ideally suited to cloud environments since the cloud has vast amounts of capacity available on demand.

However, it does not mean that the cloud has infinite capacity. The elasticity of the cloud is much higher than a traditional IT environment of an enterprise as the cloud is architected to be scalable and the cloud provider keeps enough capacity to meet the needs of its customers. Also, since it is a shared infrastructure, the peaks and troughs of usage by multiple tenants, particularly over wide geographic ranges, ensure that the infrastructure is used more optimally than a dedicated one.

Pay Per Use

The cloud providers provide metering and billing so that the customers can be billed on a pay-per-use model. The customers use the capacity and are billed for the usage. This is analogous to the way telecom companies bill their customers by the number and duration of calls made; at the end of the month, a bill is generated detailing the calls, duration, and the cost of each item. The cloud operates in a similar way where transparent billing is available based on various types of plans and customers can pay using various methods including a credit card.

Shared Management

Since the cloud provider offers a standardized mass market service, there are aspects of the service that are self-managed. The basic monitoring, provisioning, replication, and availability of service are managed by the cloud provider using advanced technologies.

The economies of scale and automation are realized in the cloud world since now it is possible for the cloud provider to provide these advanced technologies for self-managed infrastructure in a standardized fashion. The cloud provider provides basic management features and functions through automated means and the layers above are to be managed by the customer. As an example, the IaaS provider provides the virtualization platform and shared network and storage as a managed service, but the operating system and the applications run on this infrastructure by the customer have to be managed by the customer. Thus, the management of the core cloud platform is done by the provider and the other components are managed by the customers themselves.

The cloud provides cost savings and agility to enterprises and consumers so that they can focus on their core business and enjoy the benefits of a highly available and scalable service.

Next, we'll define and explain the service models in cloud computing. Figure 1-2 shows the various models and their characteristics.

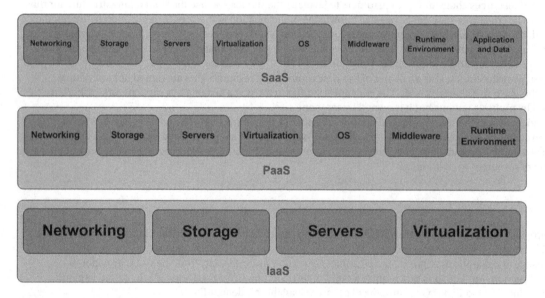

Figure 1-2. *Service models for cloud computing: IaaS, PaaS, and SaaS*

Service Models

Cloud computing service models are layers of services that the cloud provider can provide to customers. It is essential to understand the basic models in which cloud services are delivered. Different models cater to different kinds of requirements and can achieve different business objectives.

Depending on the offering and needs of the customer, they can consume pure compute resources on the cloud (which is called *Infrastructure as a Service*), or consume a platform on which applications can be written and deployed (which is called *Platform as a Service*), or leverage full-blown applications or services like e-mail from the cloud (which is termed *Software as a Service*).

Cloud Infrastructure as a Service

Infrastructure as a Service (IaaS) is the basic model where compute resources are provided to consumers on the cloud. The cloud vendor manages the data centers, network equipment, computer hardware, virtualization, and automation layers to provide the resources for customers.

In this model, the consumer is provided with on-demand computer hardware, storage, networks, and other fundamental computing resources so that the consumer can deploy and run software, which can include operating systems and applications. The consumer does not manage or control the underlying cloud infrastructure but has control over the operating system and the applications and data deployed on it. The customer may also have limited control over some of the network and security components.

Cloud Platform as a Service

The Platform as a Service (PaaS) layer is one above IaaS. In PaaS, a software platform is provided to the consumer for building and deploying applications. This platform encompasses SDKs, IDEs, and other application-specific software and frameworks like Java, .NET, and others. Developers can start development right away without wasting time on configuring and setting up the environment.

The consumer does not manage or control the underlying cloud infrastructure including network, servers, OSs, storage, or the application platform but has control over the deployed applications and possibly application hosting environment configurations. The cloud provider is responsible for upgrading the platform on a regular basis. However, the customer may need to make configuration changes or other changes to keep up with the upgrades in the underlying platform.

PaaS is a fast-evolving model, and various players include Microsoft with its Azure offering, VMware with the CloudFoundry, and Salesforce.com with its Force offering. PaaS provides a powerful medium for software developers to create applications rapidly without bothering about the underlying infrastructure elements. Some PaaS providers provide reusable libraries/components and rapid application development environments to achieve the above.

Cloud Software as a Service

Software as a Service (SaaS) is provided to the consumer to use the provider's ready-to-use applications running on a cloud infrastructure. These applications can be directly used over the Web through browsers. Examples include web-based sales management systems, office collaboration tools, payroll systems, etc. The consumer does not need to worry about underlying cloud infrastructure like network, servers, OSs, storage, or even individual application capabilities. However, the customer is responsible for limited configuration of the application settings, and configuration of users and provisioning them to use the applications features.

Deployment Models

The deployment models for the cloud cover the modes in which the cloud can be deployed and shared between organizations. Customers seeking cloud solutions must choose a deployment model for a cloud computing solution based on their specific business, operational, and technical requirements. The differences lie primarily in the scope and access of published cloud services as they are made available to service consumers. There are four primary cloud deployment models: private cloud, community cloud, public cloud, and hybrid cloud. The following sections define each of the deployment models.

Private Cloud

The private cloud infrastructure is operated solely for an organization, mostly on-premise. It may be managed by the organization or a third party and may exist on or off premise. In other words, a private cloud is a proprietary computing architecture serving a limited number of people behind the firewall to ensure desired control and management. A private cloud is generally set up on-premise within the organization's own network infrastructure. The private cloud is shared between the departments, employees, and locations of an organization and still achieves the concept of resource pooling and sharing, though in a limited fashion.

Community Cloud

The cloud infrastructure in the community cloud model is shared by several organizations and supports a specific community that has shared concerns (for example, mission, security requirements, policy, and compliance considerations.) It may be managed by the organizations or a third party and may exist on or off premises.

The community cloud is specifically tailored to meet the requirements of a particular community or type of business. As an example, government departments that have similar network, security, compute, and automation needs can come together on a government cloud, which is specifically tailored to the needs of government departments.

Public Cloud

The public cloud infrastructure is made available to the general public or a large industry group and is owned by an organization selling cloud services. The public cloud model is where the services are provided to the general public and everyone is free to subscribe to the services of the cloud provider. The services are not tailored for a specific set of customers. Examples of public cloud providers include AWS (Amazon Web Servicess), Microsoft Azure, and Rackspace.

Hybrid Cloud

A hybrid cloud, as the name suggests, is a combination of two or more of the above types of clouds. An organization may create a private cloud for applications that are tightly integrated with legacy systems and have statutory requirements to be on the premises; however, the organization may leverage the public cloud for front-end applications and may create a link between these two clouds.

A hybrid cloud may leverage the same management framework or tools. The cloud infrastructure is a composition of two or more clouds (private, community, or public) that remain unique entities but are bound together by standardized or proprietary technology that enables data and application portability (such as cloud bursting for load-balancing between clouds.) Hybrid clouds inherit the features of both private and public clouds and are primarily subjected to application criticality and customers' business needs. Figure 1-3 depicts a modern enterprise leveraging cloud services to execute end-to-end business functions.

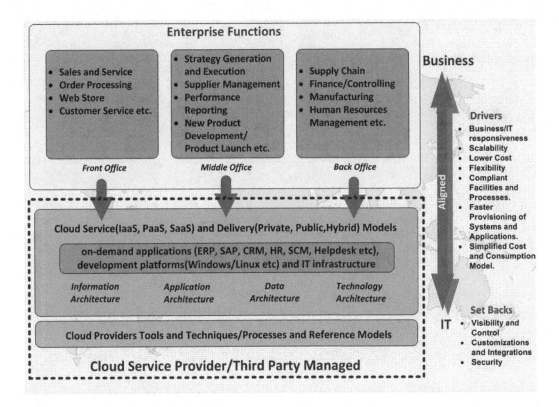

Figure 1-3. *On cloud enterprise IT*

Cloud computing has led to a paradigm shift of IT from customer, or internal IT, to eternal IT, or cloud IT, for efficiencies and business benefits in true terms.

CHAPTER 2

■ ■ ■

Cloud Stakeholders and Value Chain

This chapter casts light on the cloud/value chain and the various stakeholders that are involved in delivering cloud services. Cloud services right from creation until consumption are defined through various cloud views, such as a service-based view and a layered view. These views are the perspectives through which users see cloud services. This chapter also introduces the various stakeholders that participate in cloud services. It's important to understand the role that each stakeholder plays and the basis on which they plan, deliver, and consume cloud services. In the cloud/value chain, roles like service creators, service aggregators, and service consumers are defined. How they plan for capacity is also explained in this chapter.

Cloud Views

The cloud computing world is a marketplace that brings together the cloud consumer and the cloud provider. The relationship is more coupled and dependent on technology than the traditional vendor/client relationship.

The cloud provider provides on-demand computing resources to consumers who, at the click of a button, can order compute instances that can be quickly provisioned and configured automatically. Cloud computing is changing the way we buy and use computing resources. Rather than ordering hardware and waiting for it to get delivered and provisioned, cloud computing makes it quick and simple to access compute resources on demand.

The cloud computing model poses new challenges and fundamentally changes the way we look at capacity management. In traditional environments, complex algorithms were used to calculate and forecast the capacity requirement of an application based on how the application was developed and the number of users who would be accessing the application, plus potential demand spikes. The application development was done with the vertical server capacity in mind, including the number of cores and memory. It was not always easy to increase capacity due to constraints such as lead time to order hardware.

In the cloud computing world, it is the provider's job to see to it that there is abundant capacity available; from an enterprise perspective, the capacity can be thought of as available in abundance and on demand. Application development is done by considering the horizontal capacity available in cloud environments and the lowest unit of capacity available in the cloud environments. Thus, the application can use the elastic nature of the cloud to consume more capacity as the demand increases rather than provisioning enough capacity upfront based on estimates.

We'll now discuss the important players in the cloud computing marketplace cloud service delivery chain. The cloud computing environment brings together the cloud supplier and the cloud provider, and this is explained in the service delivery chain for cloud computing.

Before starting with the capacity management process in the cloud environments, it is important to understand the various aspects of cloud computing. A cloud environment is very dynamic and there is diversity in the roles played by the multiple stakeholders, so it is helpful to understand the scope of each. It is also helpful to understand how the cloud service value chain works and to identify the major contributors who deliver value—from the service creators to the end users.

There are multiple components that can contribute to an overall cloud service; when deployed as a hybrid cloud, it further involves multiple parties providing service within specified service levels. A multi-vendor environment has to be looked at from two standpoints. One is the consumer/supplier view, and the other is the infrastructure layer view.

Service Delivery Chain in the Cloud

The cloud marketplace has resulted in the creation of services; there are cloud service creators, cloud service aggregators, and consumers.

Cloud service creators can be players like Amazon, Microsoft, Rackspace, and EMC, who are involved in creating cloud services and infrastructure. Heavy investments are required to create cloud services as this involves procurement of infrastructure like data center facilities, racks for housing servers, power and cooling systems, storage, network components and devices, etc.

On the other hand, service aggregators provide solutions for enterprises and allow customers to pick cloud solutions according to their specific needs and budget. Service aggregators enable enterprises to use cloud services effectively and easily. They manage and aggregate services from multiple cloud creators and provide the required services to customers.

The service consumer can buy the cloud services from service aggregators or the cloud providers, depending on the need. An aggregator will provide multiple options and higher numbers of services and will typically bundle services like support and migration, while a cloud provider will provide standard services with limited support for migration.

Here's a closer look at each option.

Service-Based View

In a service-based cloud service delivery chain, the following is included (see Figure 2-1):

- Cloud service creators (cloud providers)
- Cloud service aggregators
- Consumers

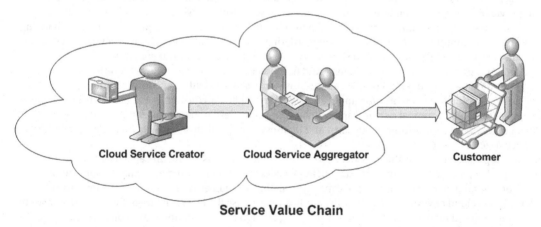

Service Value Chain

Figure 2-1. Service value chain

Cloud Service Creator

The cloud service creator defines the services that they want to offer in the cloud computing space, which could be IaaS, PaaS, or SaaS environments. The service creators define their offerings, which cover the following:

- Service definition
- Service utility and warranty

- Service geography

- Service SLAs

- Service monitoring and management, which includes monitoring, event management, availability, capacity management, problem management, and change management capabilities.

The cloud service creator provides a catalogue and one or more request portals to the aggregator or deliverer, who provides significant efficiencies and value additions to services offered in the value chain. The catalogue provides a list of the templates, the associated costs, SLAs, and delivery locations.

The cloud service provider also provides APIs to connect to the request portal and catalogue so that the cloud aggregators or cloud consumers can access these from outside systems. In addition, the cloud service provider provides metering, rating, and billing so that the consumers know the charges and their breakdown, and notifications on service availability and SLAs.

The cloud service creator's view for capacity planning is in terms of demand forecasts for infrastructure usage and business trends. Ever-growing business needs may result in procuring and crafting datacenter design in such a fashion that all capacity-related needs of cloud service aggregators and customers are fulfilled in a timely manner, no matter how large the scale of demand. This may involve procurement of storage, network devices, and associated plant expenditures, bandwidth, and computer power. Service usage data and demand management procedures assist service creators in setting up capacity-related requirements.

The complexity and scale of capacity planning for a cloud provider increases many fold since they are managing a complex and dynamic environment that typically spans multiple locations offering delivery and redundancy around the globe.

The cloud provider's margins are directly related to the capacity utilization of the cloud services offered. They also have to make sure that enough capacity is available at locations where the services are consumed and demanded. The dynamic nature of demand and the multi-tenancy aspects make this a complex process. The next few chapters will take the reader through the cloud capacity processes as applicable to a cloud provider.

Cloud Service Aggregator

The cloud service aggregator aggregates services from various cloud providers and provides a uniform way to order services and manage multiple underlying cloud providers. The cloud aggregator provisions tools and processes that work seamlessly across cloud providers and thus provide ease of use and the best-of-breed benefits to cloud consumers.

The cloud service aggregator acts as a single interface in multiple cloud providers and helps the cloud consumer leverage the strengths of various cloud providers. The cloud consumer can therefore use the aggregator to enable higher availability across cloud providers and use the IaaS, PaaS, and SaaS layers. This can be achieved by having an application deployed on multiple cloud platforms so that unavailability or an outage in one cloud provider's infrastructure doesn't impact the application—it keeps running in the other cloud provider's environment. An example of this kind of usage is to have an application hosted and running in Microsoft Azure as well as AWS.

The cloud service aggregator also aggregates the billing and provides a single bill to the cloud consumer. The cloud service aggregator provides add-on services to the consumer. The aggregator also may provide services like migration and support of multiple cloud environments. In essence, the aggregator becomes a single interface for the customer, providing unified billing and a single point of contact for availing multiple services. Jamcracker is one such company that provides cloud aggregation services. The cloud service aggregator can provide unified SLAs to the cloud consumer, offering simplified management of SLAs.

Like service creators, cloud service aggregators also plan for capacity usage and future business needs of their customers. Cost can be an important factor in planning for capacity, as there are options available when picking cloud service creators. Financial modeling can help in planning for cost-justifiable capacity. Infrastructure capacity can be procured from multiple vendors, and multiple SLAs come into action while planning for this. Customer's usage data, performance reports, and future business requirements are the major factors in efficient capacity planning.

The need for sourcing multiple services arises because different cloud providers provide different services, and an enterprise may need all of these services for their business. As an example, an enterprise may want to use Google for their e-mail services, AWS for IaaS, and Azure to host applications developed on the .NET platform; they may also use Salesforce.com as a SaaS platform for their sales and marketing requirements. An aggregator can combine all these services and provide them to the customer as a managed offering.

The cloud service aggregator works closely with the customers to understand their application and business usage to provide a tailored service to the consumer. The cloud aggregator matches the business needs, functionality, capacity, and cost requirements from the consumer to the available cloud service provider options and provides a best-of-breed solution.

Service Consumer

Service consumers seek cloud solutions from either a service creator or service aggregator in keeping with business requirements. Service aggregators seek cloud services from creators and manage various SLAs in a multi-vendor environment as a consumer. Service consumers seek cloud solutions that are a best fit in terms of maximum resource utilization and ease of management. Service consumers also seek services enabling them to migrate infrastructure to a cloud computing model that may include cloud consulting, cloud readiness assessment (for infrastructure and applications), workload assessments, cloud migration, and so on.

The customer needs to focus on business demand projections provided by the business teams, based on the demand data and the current capacity utilization of IT services. In this environment, the customer needs to model their requirements in terms of network bandwidth, computer power, and storage from an infrastructure and a service perspective. However, since the cloud model provides capacity on demand, the consumer is saved from guessing the capacity needs of the application to a large extent because the capacity can be ordered through the cloud as required. Sudden spikes in demand for capacity can now be accommodated since machines with more processor power or a greater number of machines can be provisioned in the cloud environment.

Without cloud computing, for applications hosted in a data center, sudden spikes in usage were often impossible to accommodate. As a result, capacity planning focused on taking the highest amount of capacity that remained underutilized for most periods. An example of such a scenario is a shopping cart application where capacity needs increase because of spikes in demand during holiday seasons. In a cloud computing scenario, more capacity can be provisioned during the holiday season for a few days rather than buying upfront capacity and provisioning it in the data center. Other examples are consumer-facing applications, which can get viral because of their unique features, and usage of social media tools, which can promote an application to millions of users in a single day. In such scenarios, a startup offering an application can easily leverage the cloud computing environment and serve the customers hitting their web site. In another example, an Oscar-winning movie can create huge interest in the community, and the web site of that movie may see substantial increased user activity in the days following the awards ceremony.

Applications can scale vertically or horizontally. Vertically scaling applications run on a single server and will need a bigger server to run increased workloads; this can be achieved by moving the application to a server with higher capacity. Horizontally scaling applications can span multiple servers; during increased workloads, multiple machines can be provisioned in a cloud computing environment to cater to the capacity requirements.

Application development in the cloud consumer environment uses the elasticity features of the cloud to create applications that scale up horizontally rather than vertically. The scale out approach is the preferred approach in designing applications running on cloud computing platforms. The scale out approach is so preferred that the AWS (Amazon Web Services) compute offering is called EC2 (Elastic Compute Cloud).

As an example, a small startup company may create an application and use only a single instance to host and test-market it. If the application becomes successful and many users start using it, the startup company can then buy additional capacity when the user base grows, rather than make an upfront investment in hardware capacity. For this reason, the cloud offers significant advantages to startup businesses with unknown growth cycles. This has revolutionized and democratized software development; a small group of individuals with the right idea and creativity can start creating an application using cloud computing to minimizing upfront investments.

Layer-Based View

Let's get a better understanding of the various layers of technology that form the cloud computing environment.

The cloud service is comprised of various layers, and these layers as a service are provided by cloud service creators. Figure 2-2 depicts the complete ecosystem of the cloud services models. Cloud service creators create cloud services that can be then offered in any of the service models, like SaaS, PaaS, and IaaS.

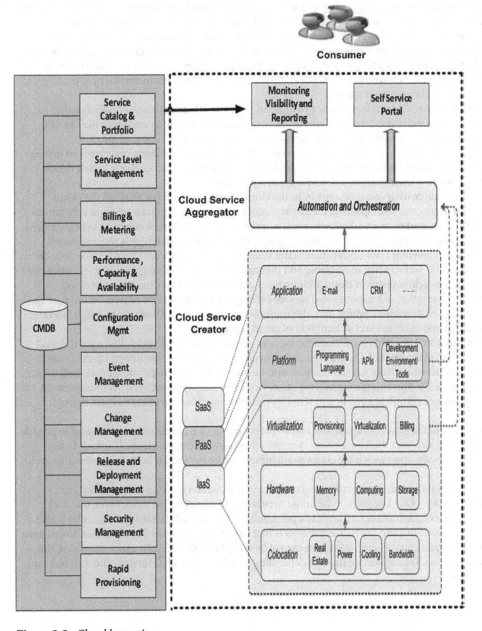

Figure 2-2. *Cloud layer view*

The bottom layer depicts the co-location facilities, which include the data center facilities, power infrastructure, cooling, and facilities such as cabling.

The hardware tier includes computer resources, storage resources, and network resources to provide the connectivity.

The virtualization tier provides the virtualization of the computer, storage, and network resources so that the same can be automated and orchestrated by the automation engine. Virtualization is a key piece that brings standardization and easy automation capabilities to the table. Virtualization is the core piece upon which cloud offerings are built.

The layer above virtualization hosts the operating system and can host the PaaS framework within the OS. The PaaS layer provides for programmability and other frameworks to create applications and deploy them on the platform.

Above the PaaS layer are applications that get created using PaaS and provide the business functions that are used by businesses. Examples of applications available as SaaS are e-mail, document management, collaboration, etc.

The automation and orchestration tier provides the integration for deploying and managing virtualization layers. The automation and orchestration tiers convert a virtualized environment into a cloud environment by providing the interface from the service request management system.

The cloud consumers use the service catalog to select virtualized templates that are provisioned using the automation engine. The catalog provides the details about the template, which can include attributes like the OS, CPU, memory, and storage along with the software that is preinstalled on the system.

Monitoring, visibility, and reporting provide views into the cloud infrastructure, and users can view and manage the virtual machines they ordered from the cloud provider or aggregator. The users can access their billing details from the visibility layer and also view their charges and consumption patterns.

The cloud consumers can source their requirements from the cloud provider directly or through the cloud aggregators. From the service aggregator's perspective, the management and automation parts become very critical in order to provide cloud solutions and carry out deployments (i.e., private clouds, public clouds, and hybrid clouds). They allow customers to provision resources like infrastructure, platform, and software through a request portal. The service catalog of a service aggregator is an aggregation of the catalogs of the underlying cloud service providers.

The cloud aggregator may add services like monitoring and management, provide a single interface to multiple clouds, and abstract the underlying differences in cloud architectures and cloud services from different cloud providers. This is enabled by the creation of templates and service catalogs that allow service aggregators to manage and control their heterogeneous environment, which includes multiple components and multiple vendors. Service offered by aggregators includes management and automation of cloud components.

The IT service management features and cloud characteristics like resource pooling, scalability, metering and billing, chargeback, hybrid cloud management, monitoring and management, and so on are integral parts of any cloud infrastructure. Along with these services a customer may also be interested in having visibility into availability of management processes and metrics on change management, service level management, security management, etc. The service aggregator must ensure complete control and visibility into customers' cloud infrastructure through a unified window.

Figure 2-2 depicts the layers of the cloud infrastructure and displays how service providers are positioned to provide the cloud services to customers at all layers. This bottom-up view helps in understanding the basic IT infrastructure the facilities require and the hardware upon which the entire cloud infrastructure pyramid is built—with virtualization technology at its heart.

Cloud service providers (creators) and aggregators use IT infrastructure, which is based on virtualization technology, to deliver cloud services. One key point to be noted here is that in any cloud service model, like IaaS, PaaS, and SaaS, the preceding service infrastructure layer is a prerequisite. For example, PaaS is based on IaaS, and SaaS is based on PaaS. The beauty of this service delivery model is that the service provider and customer do not have to worry about an underlying infrastructure layer; it is taken care of by the service provider. In many situations, the same service provider can provide all cloud service models depending on who needs what service. This can be easily understood through Figure 2-2.

CHAPTER 3

■ ■ ■

Technology that Drives the Cloud

This chapter throws some light on the technology ingredients that drive cloud computing. Before moving on to capacity management, it is essential to know what enables cloud computing and what constitutes cloud architecture. This chapter focuses on concepts like virtualization, virtual machine, cloud architecture, and so on. How these features synchronize to deliver cloud services is also described in this chapter.

Virtualization: The Engine of Cloud Computing

Virtualization technology and the breakneck speed at which computer processor technology has progressed has enabled the cloud computing environment to become viable and beneficial to customers.

The increase in CPU capacity, wherein there are multiple cores and multiple sockets in a single server, provides enough CPU and memory capacity to run multiple operating system images on a single server.

Virtualization, in computer science, is the creation of virtual (rather than actual) versions of a device or service, such as a hardware platform, OS, storage device, or network resources (Figure 3-1). Virtualization is an art of slicing the IT hardware into partitions by implementing virtualization technology or hypervisors on top of the IT hardware and converting physical infrastructure into virtual servers, virtual storage, virtual networks, etc.

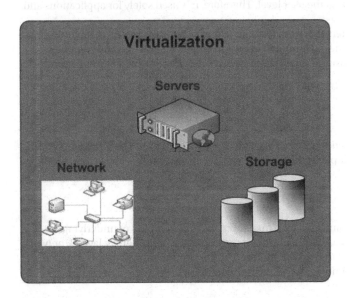

Figure 3-1. *Virtualization components*

Virtualization can be viewed as part of an overall trend in enterprise IT that includes autonomic computing (a scenario where the IT environment is able to manage itself based on perceived activity) and utility computing (where computer processing and power is seen as a utility that clients can pay for only as needed.) The usual goal of virtualization is to centralize administrative tasks while improving scalability and workloads.

Cloud computing essentially uses virtualization technologies to share a single server across multiple OS images, which may be from multiple customers. Virtualization is a key component of the cloud, but the scope of cloud computing is much more than virtualization. Keeping virtualization technology at the heart, the ability to deploy and scale infrastructure rapidly and programmatically, on-demand, on a pay-as-you-go basis—that's what really defines the cloud, and that is difficult, if not impossible, to achieve using traditional virtualization alone.

Virtual Machine

A virtual machine (VM) is a type of computer application that is used to create a virtual environment. In other words, the software simulates another environment. The creation of this virtual environment is referred to as virtualization. Virtualization allows the user to see the infrastructure of a network through a process of aggregation. Virtualization may also be used to run multiple operating systems at the same time.

There are several different types of virtual machines. Most commonly, the term is used to refer to a virtual machine that creates and runs virtual machines, also known as a hypervisor or virtual machine monitor (VMM). This type of software makes it possible to perform multiple executions on one computer. In turn, each of these executions may run an OS. This allows for a single hardware component to be used to run different operating systems and different applications, which may be used by multiple cloud customers.

Using a virtual machine lets the user have a seemingly private machine with fully functional, emulated hardware that is separate from other users. The virtual machine software also makes it possible for users to boot and restart their machines quickly, since tasks such as hardware initialization are not necessary.

A virtual machine can also refer to application software. With this software, the application is isolated from the computer being used. This VM software is intended to be used on a number of computer platforms. This makes it unnecessary to create separate versions of the same software for different OSs and computers. The Java virtual machine is a very well-known example of an application virtual machine.

A virtual machine can also be a virtual environment, which is also known as a virtual private server. A virtual environment of this type is used for running programs at the user level. Therefore, it is used solely for applications and not for drivers or OS kernels.

A virtual machine may also be a group of computers that work together to create a more powerful machine. In this type of a machine, the software makes it possible for one environment to be implemented across several computers. This makes it appear to the end user as if he or she is using a single computer, whereas there are actually numerous computers at work.

Virtual Servers

A virtual server is a virtual machine that provides functionality just like that of a physical server. The virtual server can be located anywhere and may even be shared by multiple owners.

Virtual Network

A virtual network is a pool of virtual nodes directly connected by virtual links and based on top of underlying physical resources. Virtual and physical nodes talk to each other through protocols that are generally layer 3/network layer protocols. In other words, a virtual network is a large network formed by the combination of interconnected groups of networks. Network virtualization is the technology behind virtual networks.

Virtual Storage

Virtual storage takes a combination of storage media (such as discs, tapes, etc.) and consolidates them into one storage pool, which is then provided as needed as virtual space. Storage virtualization enables cost-effective usage and resource utilization. Virtual storage is accessed by mapping the virtual addresses to physical/real addresses.

Virtual Firewall

A virtual firewall is a software appliance that regulates and controls the communication between virtual machines in a virtual environment. A virtual firewall inspects packets and uses security policy rules to block unapproved communication between VMs. Along with packet filtering, a virtual firewall can also help in providing monitoring of virtual communication between VMs.

Load Balancer

In a cloud environment, a load balancer distributes network traffic across a number of virtual servers. Load balancers are used to handle situations of concurrency and to ensure that resource capacity is utilized optimally.

Load balancers are used to improve the overall performance of applications by providing servers that are best able to perform the requested task. There are several techniques like round robin, least connection, and so on by which the load balancer decides which server should handle certain traffic or tasks.

Virtual Applications and Middleware

Virtual applications are deployed on top of virtual machines. Virtual machines are virtual images that are provided as a catalog for users to choose from and are instantiated from storage. Virtual application deployment is simpler and faster due to preinstalled and preconfigured components. Virtual machines can be used to host middleware, which enables connections of applications with other platforms, networks, and other components.

Cloud Architecture Layers

Figure 3-2 depicts the cloud architecture layers.

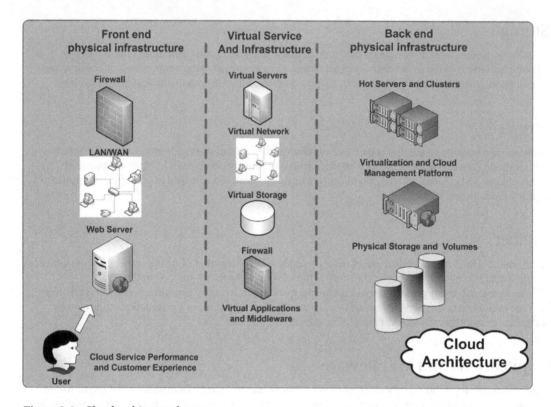

Figure 3-2. *Cloud architecture layers*

As Figure 3-2 suggests, the cloud computing layers may have networks, firewalls, and servers that lie outside the cloud environment and that are connected to the virtualized cloud infrastructure in the middle. The virtualized infrastructure is hosted on servers and storage, and it is managed by virtualization and the cloud management platform.

CHAPTER 4

■ ■ ■

Introduction to Capacity Management

After going through the basics of cloud computing and how cloud computing leverages virtualization technologies to provide pooled and shared resources to customers, let's now try to understand capacity management processes and procedures. This chapter primarily focuses on the capacity management process, its various layers and procedures.

ITIL Overview

Before understanding the capacity management process, let's have a look at the ITIL (IT Infrastructure Library) framework from which this process is derived.

As mentioned in Figure 4-1, ITIL framework version 3 consists of five documents explaining the phases that describe almost all IT projects. These phases are called the service management life cycle. The titles of these phases are

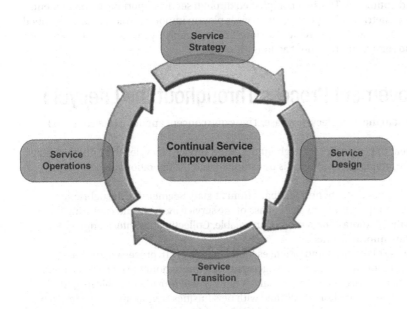

ITIL Service Lifecycle Phases

Figure 4-1. ITIL v3

- Service strategy

- Service design

- Service transition

- Service operation

- Continuous service improvement

The *service strategy* volume focuses on establishing the governance and policies around the entire IT service management effort. This may include establishing the financial process, demand management process, and service portfolio management process. The service strategy volume helps an enterprise to set the capacity-related guidelines within which service capacity is designed.

The *service design* volume specifically defines the capacity management process. Service design is the key phase of any service life cycle and it is obviously necessary to have a well-defined capacity management process to support the service. The service design volume also describes the other key elements that are part of designing an IT service, such as availability management, service continuity management, service-level management, and information security management.

The *service transition* document focuses on implementing a new service or ensuring the retirement of existing service. This is accomplished through change management and release management processes. Inputs in the form of capacity assumptions are taken into consideration when introducing a new service. Also, during service retirement, released infrastructure capacity is reclaimed for future use.

The *service operation* phase (or volume) deals with the daily management of services that are in operation. Processes such as event management, incident management, and problem management are introduced here. Failures of capacity management eventually become incidents, and insufficient capacity management is often cited as a contributing factor or even a root cause of an IT problem. The *continual service improvement* phase ensures that services are constantly improved and optimized. This is accomplished through service reporting, measurement, and improvement processes. In this phase, metrics and reporting on services play an important role and are described for all corrective actions. Capacity design inputs and improvement actions from the capacity management process are taken into account for overall process and service improvement actions.

Continual Service Improvement Process Throughout the Lifecycle

Each lifecycle phase will provide an output to the next lifecycle phase. This same concept applies to the continual service improvement (CSI) process.

An organization can find improvement opportunities throughout the entire service lifecycle. An IT organization does need to wait until a service or service management process is transitioned into the operations area to begin identifying improvement opportunities.

To be effective, the CSI process requires open and honest feedback from IT staff. Segmenting the debriefing or review into smaller, individual activities completed within each phase of the service lifecycle and capturing the lessons learned within that phase makes the plethora of data more manageable. Collecting this information is a positive beginning toward facilitating future improvements

The CSI process will make extensive use of methods and practices found in many ITIL processes, such as problem management, availability management, and capacity management used throughout the lifecycle of a service. The use of the outputs, in the form of flows, matrices, statistics, or analysis reports, will provide valuable insight into the design and operation of services. This information, combined with new business requirements, technology specifications, IT capabilities, budgets, trends, and possibly external legislative and regulatory requirements will be vital to the continual service improvement process to determine what needs to be improved, prioritize it, and suggest improvements, if required.

The CSI process on its own will not be able to achieve the desired results. It is therefore essential to leverage continual service improvement activities and initiatives at each phase of the service lifecycle. This is shown in Figure 4-2.

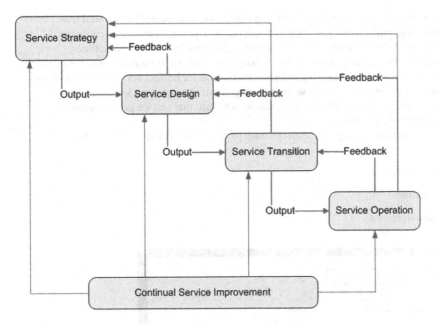

Figure 4-2. *Continual service improvement across phases*

Continual Service Improvement Feedback Mechanism

The CSI process must ensure that ITSM processes are developed and deployed in support of an end-to-end service management approach to business customers. It is essential to develop an ongoing continual improvement strategy for each of the processes as well as the services.

Integration with the Rest of the Lifecycle Stages and Service Management Processes

In order to support improvement activities, it is important to have the CSI process integrated within each lifecycle stage including the underlying processes residing in each lifecycle phase, such as

- Monitoring and data collection throughout the service lifecycle.

- Analyzing the data throughout the service lifecycle.

- Presenting and using the information throughout the service lifecycle.

The CSI process receives the collected data as input in the remainder of the continual service improvement activities.

Capacity Management Overview

The goal of the capacity management process is to ensure that cost-justifiable IT capacity, in all areas of IT, always exists and is matched to the current and future agreed-upon needs of the business, in a timely manner.

As mentioned, capacity management is one of the service design processes as defined by ITILv3. Service design is the phase of the IT service lifecycle that converts service strategy into implementable IT services. The service design phase covers principles like service availability management, capacity management, IT service continuity management, and security management. For any cloud-based service, capacity management plays a vital role in ensuring optimum resource utilization, performance, and cost effectiveness. The main purpose of capacity management is to maintain optimum and cost effective resource capacity. These resources may be facilities, hardware, software, or human resources. In addition, the capacity management process ensures the seamless launch of new IT services by providing timely resources and helping in resource forecasts for budget and planning activities.

The capacity management process works with other IT service management process areas like financial management, demand management, and service portfolio management to ensure that service performance is maintained and that you avoid running out of resources.

From a service management perspective, the capacity management process has three interrelated views (Figure 4-3):

- Business capacity management

- Service capacity management

- Component capacity management

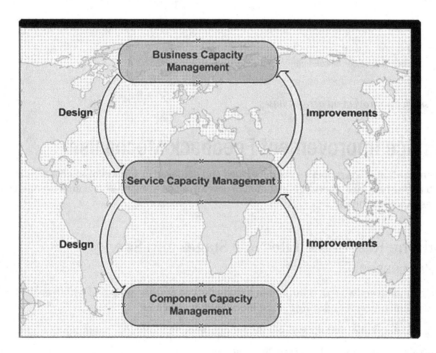

Figure 4-3. *Capacity management layers*

This distinction is made in order to achieve capacity management objectives at different levels. Capacity management process areas have to cater to different layers of capacity management. For example, determining overall capacity requirement subprocesses or procedures in the capacity management process that focus on business capacity management, rather than the other two capacity layers (service capacity and component capacity).

We will discuss these procedures in detail in later chapters. These three capacity layers have dynamic interaction with each other. As an example, capacity design inputs are translated down the hierarchy from business requirements to service requirements to component level requirements. On the other hand, improvement inputs (cost optimization and performance improvement) flow from the component level up to the business level. Capacity management takes a cyclic approach wherein business needs flow from top to bottom and performance and optimization feedback moves from bottom to top.

A cloud provider also may seek business capacity requirements from customer surveys and performance optimization reports to enhance the business service performance, features, and scope. In addition, these inputs can also be captured by analyzing the service requests that can be in the form of requests for new features or higher performance (more RAM, CPU, etc.). A cloud provider can update its service catalog on the basis of frequent service requests and ensure the customer is served with the right service at the right time. Figure 4-4 showcases how business and IT requirements converge to create the service catalog.

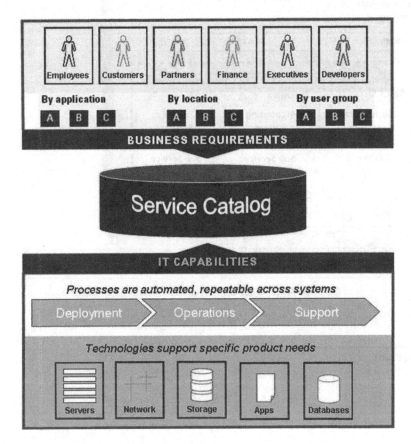

Figure 4-4. *Service catalog requirements*

The service catalog ties the business requirements to the underlying technology layers to provide a business-facing catalog of services that is used by the customers and users to order services from a service provider.

As an example, suppose the cloud consumers are requesting more complex configurations of CPU and RAM in a machine/server, or the customers are requesting servers with high configurations of RAM and solid state disks as storage to run in-memory databases. The cloud provider, seeing this type of business demand and the technology shift, follows service management processes to provide the required capacity in the form of new catalog items in the service.

Service catalog management seeks inputs from business units that consume IT services. This allows the business to do catalog-based IT service provisioning. As described in Figure 4-5, various businesses seek IT services and subservices. These subservices meet specific business or ERP-related needs. All live services are listed in the IT service catalog. Other catalogs, known as business catalogs, contain business centric information, service levels, pricing, etc. We will remain focused on IT service catalogs only for the purpose of this publication. The "ingredients" on an IT service catalog are listed in Table 4-1.

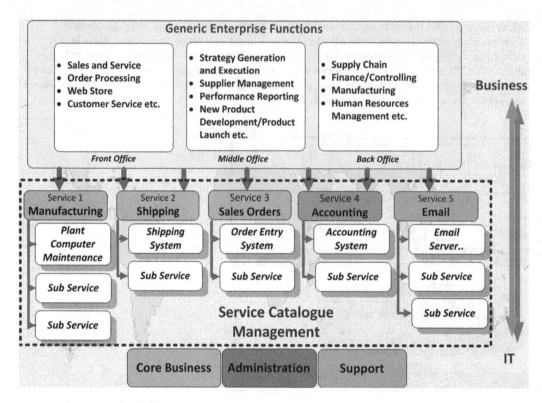

Figure 4-5. *IT service catalog*

Table 4-1. *Sample Catalog Ingredients*

Core Business Purpose: Manufacturing Plant	
Service	Contact
Computer-operated Machinery	
Inventory Program	
Shop Floor Computer Hardware Support	
Core Business Purpose: Shipping & Receiving	
Service	Contact
Order System	
Shipment Tracking	
Computer Hardware Support	
Inventory System	

(*continued*)

Table 4-1. (*continued*)

Administrative Role: Accounting Department

Service	Contact
Desktop Support	
Salary Software	
Computer Hardware Support	

Support Role: Company E-mail

Service	Contact
E-mail Exchange Server	
Network Infrastructure	

Figure 4-6 is the catalog of the Amazon Web Services (AWS) infrastructure service. This infrastructure may include CPU power, memory, storage, and an operating system running on top. This type of simplistic and flexible IT catalog helps capacity planners design and plan for optimized capacity using appropriate and cost-effective infrastructure units. In Figure 4-6, the cloud customer can request an instance of various configurations. Reserved instances are cheaper when compared with on-demand instances as there is a minimum 1 year provisioning commitment involved in reserved instances.

Linux | **Windows**

Light Utilization Reserved Instances

Region: US East (N. Virginia)

	1 yr Term		3 yr Term	
	Upfront	Hourly	Upfront	Hourly
Standard Reserved Instances				
Small (Default)	$69	$0.059 per Hour	$106.30	$0.051 per Hour
Medium	$138	$0.118 per Hour	$212.50	$0.103 per Hour
Large	$276	$0.235 per Hour	$425.20	$0.204 per Hour
Extra Large	$552	$0.47 per Hour	$850.40	$0.408 per Hour
Second Generation Standard Reserved Instances				
Extra Large	$607	$0.504 per Hour	$935	$0.432 per Hour
Double Extra Large	$1214	$1.008 per Hour	$1870	$0.864 per Hour
Micro Reserved Instances				
Micro	$23	$0.014 per Hour	$35	$0.012 per Hour
High-Memory Reserved Instances				
Extra Large	$353	$0.29 per Hour	$548	$0.245 per Hour
Double Extra Large	$706	$0.58 per Hour	$1096	$0.49 per Hour
Quadruple Extra Large	$1412	$1.16 per Hour	$2192	$0.98 per Hour

Figure 4-6. *AWS EC2 catalog (light utilization)*

While designing for optimized capacity, the business demand and fluctuations in demand are taken into consideration. For example, in a cloud environment, if a business application is not being used, the virtual machine should automatically be shut down so that the customer doesn't have to pay for unused capacity. All this should be determined when designing for capacity in a cloud environment. The interrelation between different layers of capacity must be well established, and these layers must be synchronized to fulfill the objective of overall capacity management, which is to provide cost-justifiable capacity in a timely manner.

Capacity Management Activities

Capacity management involves both proactive and reactive activities. Here is a list of some of the *proactive* activities:

- Taking actions on performance issues before they occur.

- Forecasting the future capacity requirements by trending and utilization analysis.

- Modeling and trending the predicted changes in IT services, and identifying the changes that need to be made to service.

- Ensuring that upgrades are budgeted, planned, and implemented before SLAs and service targets are breached or performance issues arise.

- Tuning and optimizing the performance of services and components.

Reactive activities include

- Reviewing the current performance of both services and components.

- Reacting to and assisting with specific performance issues.

- Responding to all capacity-related threshold events and instigating corrective action.

A Balancing Act

Capacity management is essentially a balancing act that ensures that the capacity and the performance of the IT services in an organization are utilized in a most cost effective and timely manner. These actions include

- Balancing costs against resources needed.

- Balancing supply against demand.

This balancing becomes a key parameter that is required to successfully run a cloud service. Thus, the cloud provider is required to have enough capacity to fulfill the varying on-demand needs of the customer while making sure that waste of resources is minimized and over-provisioning of capacity is kept to the minimum. This is a technology and analytics challenge that every cloud provider has to face to provide services in a competitive environment. If the cloud provider runs out of capacity, the provider runs the risk of losing customers or worse, and if the cloud provider provisions huge extra capacity, the cost of service will go up and the provider runs the risk of not being competitive in pricing.

Capacity Management: Scope and Coverage

Figure 4-7 depicts a capacity management process view that most of the enterprises follow while designing their service capacity. In the traditional model, the capacity management process takes input from other service management process areas like demand management for demand patterns and forecasts, service level management for agreed service performance-related data, change management for service change requests, etc. On the basis of these inputs, capacity requirements in terms of data center space, virtual resources like servers, network bandwidth, and storage requirements including underlying infrastructure are determined. All components required to support a business service are gathered as a first step.

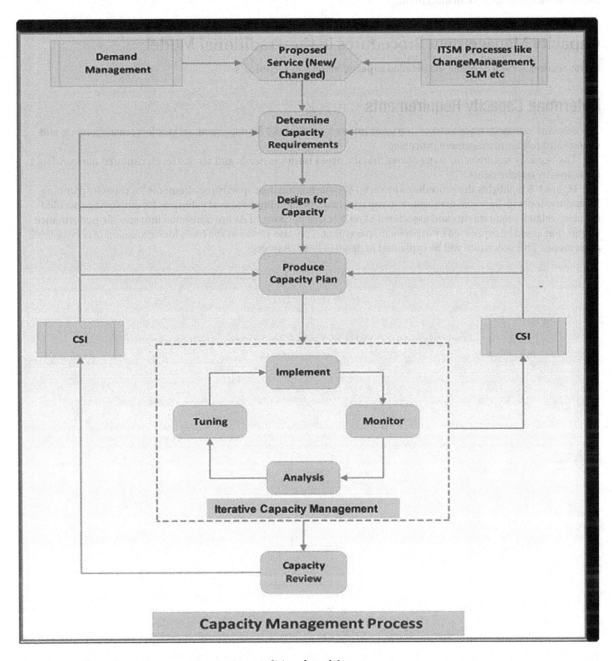

Figure 4-7. *Capacity management process in a traditional model*

As mentioned, Figure 4-7 showcases the capacity management process. This process starts with gathering capacity-related requirements from various other ITSM processes, designing for capacity, and formulating capacity design into a formal capacity plan. This capacity plan is used to store all capacity-related information during implementation of iterative management.

Capacity Management Procedures in the Traditional Model

In this section, we will describe the detailed capacity management process.

Determine Capacity Requirements

The *determine capacity requirements* step takes inputs from demand management, service level management, and change and release management processes.

The *capacity requirements* step ensures that the user's business needs and service levels captured are translated into capacity requirements.

Figure 4-8 highlights the procedures involved in determining the capacity requirements for capacity planning. In conjunction with financial management, capacity management provides cost estimates for employing specified capacity-related requirements and associated SLAs. For this purpose, SLAs are translated into specific performance targets that are to be supported by capacity management. This also serves as the basis for negotiation of service level agreements. This procedure will be explained in detail in later chapters.

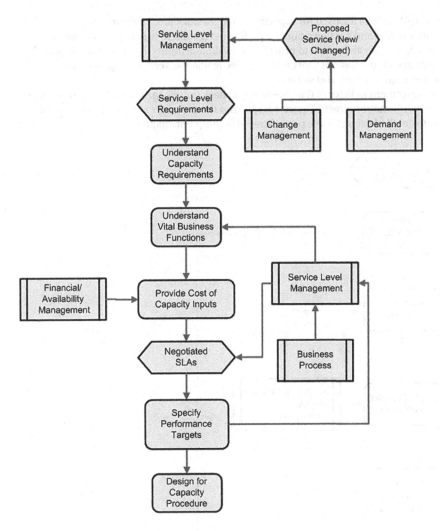

Figure 4-8. *Determining capacity requirements*

Design for Capacity

After this, the architecture of the design for the expected capacity requirements is developed. The capacity design team formulates an IT infrastructure design (consisting of all components) required to fulfill certain performance targets. This procedure is most critical and determines the success or failure of the capacity management process.

Based on the performance targets, a high-level plan to meet the targets is chosen. For example, a stiff cost focus in the performance targets might call for a just-in-time solution whereas service continuity-related requirements and stiff performance targets might require solutions that include the availability of margin capacity.

During capacity design, one or more of techniques, such as component failure impact analysis and management of risk, are used to optimize capacity design. Various statistical algorithms can also be used to establish levels of component capacity for storage, networks, and servers. Resilience design also is established on the basis of disaster recovery needs. For example, capacity requirements may double in scenarios where another disaster recovery (DR) site is in consideration.

Design considerations like the use of clusters are used for capacity design. Besides this, component-level specifications like make, model, vendor name, and configuration are performed to adhere to service performance targets. Supplier/vendor management teams are also called to provide their valuable inputs in support of this activity. Hence efficient capacity design is finalized on the basis of aspects like service resilience, security requirements, performance specifications, availability requirements, and so on.

In conjunction with financial management policies of the enterprise, a check is done for available cost reduction measures without compromising the performance targets. Figure 4-9 specifies the *design for capacity* procedure for capacity management. We will go into detail of each of these procedures in subsequent chapters.

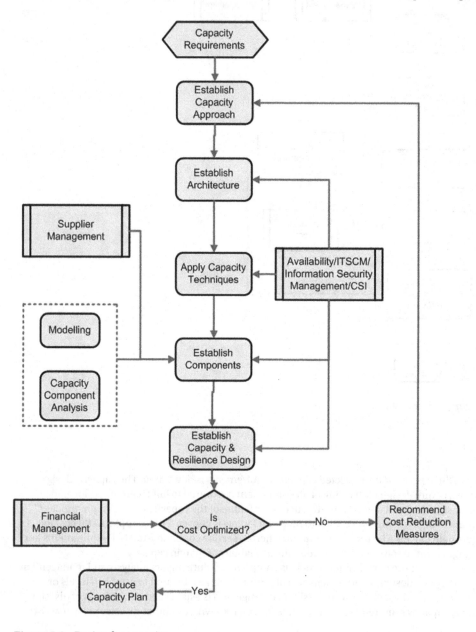

Figure 4-9. *Design for capacity*

Capacity Management Procedures in the Cloud Model

In cloud scenarios, the design for capacity takes a different approach. One of the focuses of Chapter 5 will be a look at how the cloud affects the traditional approach. For now we will look at the changes in the cloud computing model from a service consumer's perspective via the following:

- Designing applications to use the minimum capacity and ideally to scale out rather than scale up.

- Designing applications to provide metrics on usage so that new instances of the application can be instantiated up depending upon the workload from an application perspective.

- Design applications that do not rely on memory on a single server or instances for things like session state.

- Design applications that are mindful of the limits of storage input/output operations per second (IOPS) for some cloud providers.

- Design applications where the database can also work on multiple systems using read replicas and thus provide scalability.

- Design applications keeping in mind multi-regional disaster recovery to take care of disaster recovery aspects. Various cloud providers have different options available for disaster recovery.

- Design for backup and restore. The way backups work in certain cloud provider environments is different. When designing for capacity, this issue needs to be kept in mind.

- Design for network usage on public cloud providers. The network costs can be significant when leveraging cloud services, and this aspect needs attention.

Produce Capacity Plan

On the basis of capacity requirements and design specifications, a formal capacity plan is developed to address all aspects related to capacity management; this is documented and shared among all stakeholders. The capacity plan is the source of information related to all capacity requirements like scalability, adaptability, component capacity architecture, etc. The capacity plan should be maintained and reviewed periodically to ensure that information is up to date as per the current and future capacity-related requirements. Figure 4-10 describes the activities involved in producing a capacity plan.

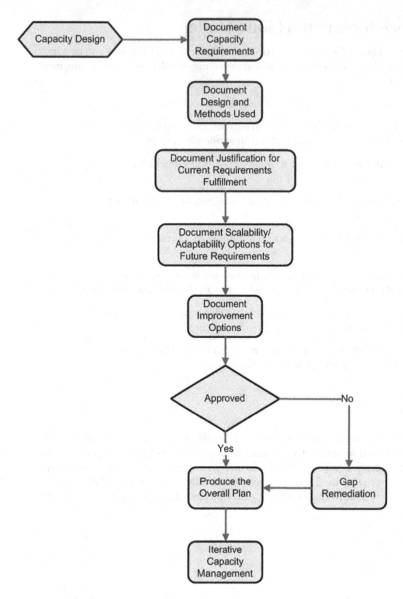

Figure 4-10. *Produce capacity plan*

Refer to subsequent chapters for capacity planning and the appendix for a capacity plan template.

Iterative Capacity Management for Live Services

After the capacity design and plan is finalized for new services, it moves into production, and here capacity management takes a different approach altogether. We can call this *iterative capacity management,* and this involves implementing the capacity plan, monitoring the service performance, analyzing the utilization reports, and tuning the capacity for ongoing improvements and handling performance fluctuations. Capacity management here is more focused on capacity optimization and performance management.

The four phases of ongoing/iterative capacity management can be summarized as

1. Implementation
2. Monitoring
3. Analysis
4. Tuning

These will be discussed in the following pages.

Implementation

The objective of this phase is to adopt a structured approach toward implementation of the capacity plan by identifying all implementation requirements and impact areas. Any capacity addition/removal/reconfiguration is evaluated in terms of its impact on current service operations. Any requirements in terms of technical configuration, procurement of hardware and software, cost of implementation, licensing requirements, and skills required for implementation are identified to achieve the desired objective of the proposed implementation of the project. Monitoring and reporting requirements are also identified and formulated here. After this, a plan of detailed activities to be performed is created; the sequence, relationship, effort and time required are developed for the proposed implementation of the project.

Monitoring the Plan

This phase is focused around measuring and reporting of performance-related capacity aspects. All activities in this phase are preferably performed by automated mechanisms. Capacity and performance monitoring on a real-time basis are performed in the event management process or monitoring tools. The event management process utilizes input from capacity management for designing the event management system (thresholds, parameters, etc.) that forms the basis of real-time monitoring. Monitoring of identified aspects of capacity over a specified performance period is covered under the scope of this phase.

Analysis

The objective of this phase is to translate the data from capacity monitoring into information that can be used to draw inferences for suggesting improvements or identifying issues. Depending on the type of modeling being conducted, performance data from monitoring is translated into a form that can be used as an input to the model.

Data reported to functional capacity owners is trended and analyzed using statistical tools. These reports are then used for decision making on capacity tuning and optimization actions. This may include reports on thresholds, consistent lack of capacity, incorrect configuration, unusual load patterns, etc.

Tuning

The tuning phase in capacity management deals with identification of solutions for fulfillment of capacity management objectives.

Workload profiles of various services are created; these include the components providing a service and the workload that these components are servicing. The workload profile provides insights into how the service and various components underneath are performing under various scenarios.

The analysis reports, which are an output of the analysis phase, are used in the tuning phase to tune the monitoring for capacity. The actions for tuning could be adding new parameters for monitoring, addition of new reports, and changing thresholds for services or components.

All changes follow the change management processes and are implemented after approvals.

Capacity Review

Lastly, a capacity management review is done wherein capacity reports are generated and presented to all stakeholders at the business, service, and component levels. All the findings and post-review actions are again fed into capacity management procedures for continual improvements.

Weekly/monthly reviews may occur in which a review of performance for capacity aspects is conducted. Actual values of performance parameters such as these are compared against the expected and target values:

- Component capacity parameters like disk, server, memory utilizations, etc.

- Service capacity parameters like e-mail service uptime, performance, etc.

- Business capacity parameters like the increase/decrease in the number of business users, etc.

- Process key performance indicators

- Process integration

- Previous periodic action items

- Data from other processes that impacts capacity (i.e. Incident/problem/change data)

Deviations are discussed and analysis is done.

On the basis of the capacity review, the resulting update items for the capacity plan are documented. The capacity plan is updated when all the documented points get the necessary approvals.

As discussed earlier, capacity management layers include resource- or component-level capacity management, service-level management, and business-level capacity management for all services and servers. Capacity management takes care of IT capacity at all three layers wherein capacity needs are fulfilled from top to bottom.

Business-oriented capacity requirements are first translated to service-related needs. Subsequently, service-related parameters are mapped with the underlying component layer that supports the IT service. In later chapters, we will explore various capacity management layers and associated procedures in detail.

CHAPTER 5

■ ■ ■

Cloud Capacity Management

Let's see how capacity management is done in cloud environments. The previous chapter introduced the capacity management process. This chapter introduces capacity planning and management at various layers: business, service and component capacity. If we try to put the benefits of cloud computing in simpler terms, it would be "optimized resource utilization and cost savings"; which coincide with the goals and objectives of capacity management. In this chapter emphasis has been given to what constitutes the capacity management process and how various cloud stakeholders perceive capacity management. This chapter also explains that how the capacity management process can be applied to cloud computing to generate infrastructure economies and optimizations.

Capacity Management in Cloud Computing

In this publication, emphasis has been given on implementing capacity management procedures and activities that are specifically designed for cloud environments. Implementing capacity management can be complex and expensive due to heterogeneous and complex infrastructure and the associated toolsets. Now let's see how capacity management processes are planned and brought into practice in cloud based environments.

In a cloud environment, service providers have to plan for managing their data center capacity and ensure the highest levels of service performance and continuity.

Inputs for determining capacity requirements are taken from tools that monitor resource performance, business trends, other cloud service management processes like service demand management, service level management, service portfolio management, and change management.

The cloud introduces aspects of multi tenancy and shared infrastructure which are leased or rented rather than being bought and, as we discussed earlier, it changes the way capacity management is done.

Redefined process interfaces will be required for enterprises who wish to use the pay as you go model and the elasticity model offered in the cloud, to effectively manage the capacity of the cloud.

For a service consumer, closer links with enterprise financial management will be the key to understanding the costs associated with the various options public, private, hybrid, etc. and using this information to assess which will best meet the needs of the business. The determination of these costs and sizing the environment correctly will be critical in ensuring that using the cloud actually pays back businesses as expected.

Let's consider a real life scenario wherein a business requires some high end servers to host a few applications for one year. Also consider the server utilization scenarios wherein servers can be utilized at low, medium, and high rates.

To keep this simple let's take one server and compare the cost of conventional DC hosting versus public cloud hosting. Scenario A (Figure 5-1) gives the hosting cost of a high end server. To keep this simple we are not counting other cost elements in DC hosting environment like space, power, and rack.

Scenario A

Vendor Name: Data Center	
DC Hosting Cost Components **1 Large Instance (7.5 GB, 4 ECU, 850 GB HDD)**	
Essential Components	**Cost $ (yearly)**
Space	
Power	
Rack	
Compute	7548
Network	
Bandwidth	
Storage	
Set up	
Maintenance	
Top Up	
Support	
OS	
Security	
Monitoring	
Total Cost	**7548**

Figure 5-1. *Traditional Server Based Model*

Scenario B

(Figure 5-2) shows the cost required to host the same server on a public cloud. Cost elements include onetime upfront costs and yearly hosting.

Provider Name: Public Cloud	
Cloud provider cost elements 1 Large Instance (7.5 GB, 4 ECU, 850 GB HDD)	
Essential Components	**Cost $ (yearly)**
Option1: Enter Overall cost	
Consolidated Cost (Source: Website)	4204.8
Option 2: Enter component-wise break up	
CPU	
Memory	
Storage	
I/O Performance	
NW Bandwidth	
OS	
Monitoring	
Upfront Cost	500
Total Cost	4704.8

Figure 5-2. *Cloud Based Server Model*

Considering above two scenarios, cost economy can easily be seen in Figure 5-3. Cloud hosting is generally much more economical than DC hosting for variable workloads. These cost figures are in US dollars.

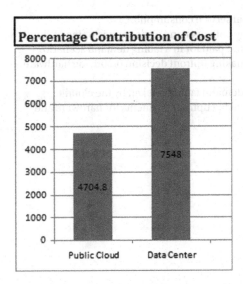

Figure 5-3. *Cost split. Cloud vs. DC hosting*

The Capacity-Utilization Curve

The graphic in Figure 5-4 illustrates capacity versus utilization.

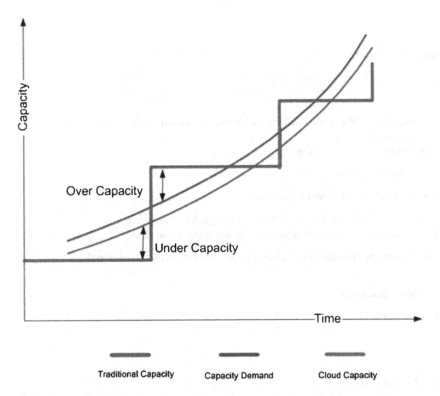

Figure 5-4. *Capacity versus utilization*

This curve shows the core themes around cloud services versus actual service consumption.

It is important to understand that cloud economies can be affected by both over and under provisioning of cloud resources. From an enterprise perspective, once the hardware is bought and paid for in a falling demand scenario there will be excess capacity which will go waste. Also the organizations making upfront decision on buying hardware are taking a risk of scenarios of falling demand.

In a cloud model the risk of technology getting obsolete or business demand falling is taken by the cloud provider. From a financial management perspective the organization is making upfront payments for hardware and thus cost of capital needs to be factored for the life the hardware.

Thus to sum up:

Cost in a traditional model will be a summation of following:

- Cost of data center facilities including hosting, power etc.

- Server hardware

- Network equipment

- Storage hardware

- Software components and licenses

- Annual maintenance for hardware and software

- Implementation or provisioning / implementation

- Network bandwidth

- Operations and maintenance

- Operating system

- Virtualization software

- Monitoring and management software

- Operations resources

- Cost of capital

The above costs need to be factored in for the life of the hardware which is dependent on the organization's hardware refresh policy and typically is around 4 years.

From a cloud model perspective the costs can be as follows:

- Upfront cost for reserving or booking instances

- Cost of pay per use compute, storage and network resources

- Cost of transactions (IOPS / GET / PUT). This is a cost that is not applicable in a private datacenter model and hence organizations need to look out for per transaction charges.

- Network bandwidth cost (this can be substantially higher in a cloud scenario than traditional scenario)

- Cost of migration to a cloud environment

- Monitoring and management tools

- Operations expenses

- Software licenses

- License migration costs (if applicable)

- Applicable annual maintenance fees

- Cost of capital

Apart from the above the risk of technology getting obsolete and the risk of downsizing are important aspects which need to be looked into to do a comparison of cloud with traditional options.

A projection of costs from the cloud model over the refresh cycle of hardware will provide the cost comparison between cloud and traditional environments.

However the above model is simplistic in nature and the following complexities need to be addressed:

- Cost reduction by cloud providers over the period. This is an important aspect as cloud providers are known to reduce costs every few months and these can be significant reductions.

- Sunk cost of hardware and software which has been already procured.

- Cost of hardware or software which will remain in the data center post migration to cloud.

- Cost of shared services which are needed in a hybrid cloud. What portion of these will get apportioned to the cloud infrastructure.

- Changes in hardware refresh policy. What happens if an organization decides to change the hardware refresh cycle from 4 years to 5 years.

Conventional vs. Cloud View of Capacity Management

Figure 5-5 below depicts the high level private cloud architecture/model which is built upon hardware infrastructure, virtualization and automation/orchestration layers.

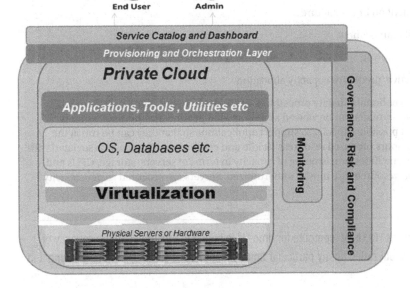

Figure 5-5. *Private Cloud Reference Model*

As discussed in earlier, Private Cloud is one of the preferred cloud deployment models amongst SMBs and Large enterprises. Typically cloud service providers to these enterprises undertake building their private cloud on the basis of application readiness and budget in hand to move applications onto the cloud. Cloud enablement includes building and configuring the hardware infrastructure, implementing virtualization technology and orchestration/automation layer.

There may be scenarios wherein the customer already has hardware and sometimes a virtualized environment; in this situation the cloud provider takes over from the current state of hardware infrastructure and transforms the environment into a cloud based set up. This is accomplished by infrastructure virtualization and orchestrating the environment and bringing in cloud computing characteristics like resource pooling, scalability, metering, billing, chargeback, and networked access.

As discussed, virtualization is the key enabler to ensure highly optimized resource utilization from cloud providers. Components of a cloud environment can be data center facilities, chassis, hardware, virtual machines, network devices, bandwidth, virtual discs, geographic regions, failure-insulated zones, archival storage and so on.

In a cloud environment, capacity management must be able to address the following issues:

- Ease of provisioning capacity leading to over-provisioning and issues like VM sprawl.

- A self-service portal makes it harder to forecast capacity demand.

- Inefficient and complex chargeback mechanisms due to multi tenant hosting in a resource-sharing environment.

- Dynamic infrastructure causes manual allocation inefficiencies and is prone to errors.

In order to do effective planning, the service provider and customer can work hand in hand and plan for future capacity. Cloud providers can provide performance and trending of capacity utilization through monitoring toolsets. Cloud customers can share business demands and expansion plans. This helps arriving at the right capacity requirements that can meet the performance requirements and support business Cloud providers need to adopt a holistic and service-oriented approach to capacity management that includes both technical and non-technical metrics, strong focus on the following:

- Optimized workload placement on infrastructure

- Dynamic capacity threshold management

- Application performance monitoring

- Real time analytics for proactive/predictive capacity allocation

Now let's try to understand how conventional capacity procedures are adapted to the cloud based model. Capacity management in traditional environments can be viewed as a somewhat pessimistic approach as there has been a focus on providing the highest possible capacity to support applications so that they can be run at the desirable level in peak hours. In off peak hours procured resources sit idle and continue to incur costs associated with datacenter space, cooling, power etc. This includes provisioning of capacity in terms of servers, storage, CPUs and network bandwidth sufficiently and these resources are mostly underutilized. Servers are procured as per capacity requirements.

 For example an enterprise seeking "x" CPUs of compute for time "t" is bound to procure compute capacity of more than "x" CPUs irrespective of utilization at any particular time. Similar issues come up with networking and storage requirements.

Thus, there is capacity waste and underutilization in the traditional way capacity is allocated. The conventional approach to capacity management clearly is not fully applicable in cloud based environments as these may bring in cost inefficiencies and operational challenges posed by dynamic virtual infrastructure environments and multiple cloud deployment models.

In modern and highly virtual/cloud environments, an IT enterprises needs to relook at its capacity management strategy which now goes beyond basic infrastructure elements like server, storage and network. There is a need to focus on application performance and its deep integration with the management stack. The new age capacity solution must be able to offer a holistic and complete view of the infrastructure resources like storage, network, server, virtual machines etc. In addition, these solutions must present a deep dive view into the individual infrastructure resources. Capacity metrics and generated capacity solutions must be able to simulate multiple usage scenarios, forecast capacity consumption, perform proactive capacity allocation etc. Modern capacity solutions must also have capability to adhere to compliance and regulatory rules whenever workload placement decisions are made.

In the new age of cloud computing the focus can shift to providing the smallest possible unit of capacity to support an application. Design of the application itself is done in such a way that minimum resources are utilized.

In capacity planning and design, we look at the lowest units of capacity available from a cloud provider rather than design for a scaled up application. Smallest possible capacity would bring in cost economies and flexibility to the consumer. For example in cloud based service offering like IaaS, one can configure a service catalog that includes server units with specifications as small as 2 GB RAM, 2 CPU, 40 GB HDD. The advantage of having small capacity units is to bring in cost efficiency and make sure that optimum resources are provided to run workloads. Also, as per the customer requirements, one can configure an IaaS service catalog with specifications of choice that can span minimal to maximum possible configurations. Along with this, the pay as you go model can save big bucks by helping enterprises reduce their TCO.

 Another example in this area would be the database as a service offering. Here the cloud provider can provide database services based on reads and writes that the customer's application may need. Thus to begin with, the customer can buy X reads and Y writes and as the application scales up to more users and usage the customer can dynamically increases the reads and writes. The customer only pays for the reads and writes allocated by the cloud provider. The cloud provider's orchestration and automation layers take care of provisioning of the required infrastructure and scaling up the database to meet the needs of the customer.

Compare the above scenario with capacity planning in a traditional model. In a traditional model the inputs for capacity of a database will be gathered beforehand in a manner similar to the following example:

Demand Management:

Demand management will provide the following data.

- The application will scale from 10 users in development environment to 1000 users during stress testing.

- The application will scale from 0 peak users in off hours to 100 peak users on weekdays and 1000 users during month end.

Service Levels:

- Availability of Service: 99.5%.

- Performance: Response time to end users of less than 5 seconds per transaction.

Now in a traditional capacity planning scenario, the hardware requirements will be based on the peak workload which is 1000 users since the service levels do not define or accept lower service levels for peak usage. Thus capacity which is 10 times of the average capacity has to be provided for, or provisioned, based on the business demand and the service levels.

In a cloud environment, the smallest possible unit for capacity is reduced from the full hardware stack to a flexible virtual server which can be used as per the utility model and would incur cost only when used.

Moreover, if an application consumes more resources, cloud computing provides scalable infrastructure which can be provisioned in minutes as compared to weeks in traditional environments. This will ensure not only that the performance of any new or changed service meets its expected targets, but also that all existing services continue to meet all of their targets.

A detailed understanding of the business needs and drivers and again how these will relate to services and infrastructure is essential in a cloud environment, and to a lesser degree, any large scale virtualization project. Achieving this level of maturity and integration presents a considerable challenge for a capacity management team, but if achieved, will benefit both the business and raise the profile of capacity management immeasurably.

If one decomposes the cloud model, it becomes clear that there are many variations on the theme and that certain variations provide more initial value than others. For example: Clouds can provide raw IaaS, higher-level PaaS (which includes pre-packaged database and middleware stacks), and even complete SaaS (which is familiar to users of sales force automation or office productivity tools over the Internet.)

On the basis of considerations like service levels, application workload and behavior, processor, I/O analysis etc there are several implication of cloud service models on the capacity management process. Now, let's try to understand what various layers of capacity management must be considered for overall capacity planning.

Business Capacity Management in Cloud

The goal of business capacity management is to ensure profitable business continuity.

Applications that are critical to the business are mapped with services supporting the business, business goals and capacity planning to ensure the business is provided with the required capacity and service levels.

Capacity management at this level must ensure application performance metrics are in place and these are tuned for the needs of business processes. Capacity utilization levels related to application-level performance must be defined, monitored and validated in a timely manner.

The focus of this aspect of capacity management is to translate business needs and plans into requirements for services and IT infrastructure, ensuring that future business requirements for IT services are quantified, designed, planned, and implemented in a timely manner. Business capacity management is a relatively long term view of capacity management as this may involve analyzing business workloads such as department wide IT usage and accordingly defining service levels to accommodate demand.

Figure 5-6 showcases how demand activities are formulated into capacity requirements. Business strategy, in conjunction with financial management, form the business plan and process. On the basis of business activity and processes, demand inputs are fed into the capacity management process.

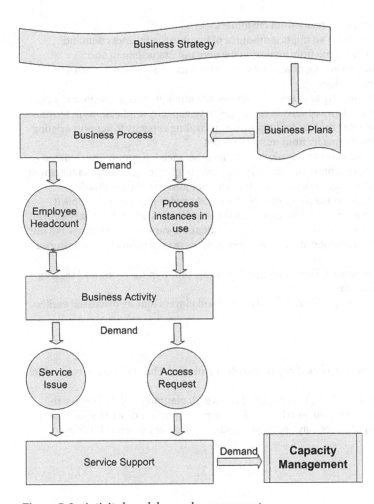

Figure 5-6. *Activity based demand management*

When cloud providers *(service creators and service aggregators)* began to offer a SaaS model, they added end-user experience monitoring to track transaction response time. The intent of this was to capture business requirements in terms of service usage and business relevance. In other words, business capacity management seeks business inputs for anticipated business needs and seeks business demand information proactively from existing business service warranty and utility measures.

The service warranty ensures that a service is fit for use while utility ensures a fit for purposes of the service.

A cloud provider may seek business capacity requirements from a number of sources including surveys, usage trends, CSAT scores and performance optimization reports to enhance the business service performance, features and scope.

This data can also be captured by analyzing the service request types which will determine who is ordering what and what is the frequency of orders.

Another input can be request for enhancements to service from customers.

Competitive analysis of competitive products is also an important source of input to the business demand.

The future requirements from business demand come from analyzing the demand management and service portfolio. This analysis should offer detail concerning new processes and service requirements, changes, improvements, and also the growth in the existing services.

A service portfolio primarily is comprised of three types of services: the service pipeline, existing services (from the service catalog) and retired services. These three types of service categories have capacity implications in terms of providing optimized capacity infrastructure to services that are in the pipeline, providing capacity to support existing services in the service catalog, and freeing allocated capacity from retired services.

Business capacity management ensures that demand for supply of capacity is balanced. If supply and demand were out of balance, this would directly impact the cost of service delivery. To perform effective capacity management, organizations need to monitor application infrastructures, end-user experience, and infrastructure utilization over time to gauge that sufficient capacity exists to meet the requirements of agreed service levels. For example if a business goal is to have efficient collaboration and communication within the organization, underlying services can be email, chat, portals and wikis etc. Each of these services can in turn be dependent on various components like the network and storage. So capacity planning needs to be done at all levels to ensure the overall business is running on cost justifiable capacity.

Prime business capacity management activities would be trending, forecasting, prototyping, sizing and seeking ongoing inputs to predict future business requirements.

Let's discuss how business capacity management plays a role in all three cloud players that we discussed earlier:

Cloud Service Provider

The cloud service provider is in the business of providing cloud capacity to its consumers. The cloud is a service which is offered by the cloud service providers.

The financial management aspects of offering services are considered for overall planning of the business, the capacity to be offered at various locations and for the various service portfolio items. Figure 5-7 describes the generic procedure to capture the business trends. Cloud providers may use these trends to carry out pattern of business activity analysis.

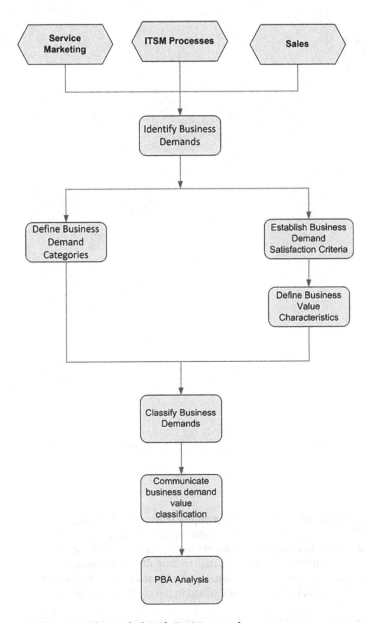

Figure 5-7. *Value and Classify Business needs*

Pattern of business activity (PBA): Patterns of business activity are used to help the IT service provider understand and plan for different levels of business activities. As part of the demand management process the concept of patterns of business activity is the primary source of information regarding anticipated service demand. These activities can be in the form of service enhancement, expansion or any other modification. For example, a customer may introduce a service in new geographies, increase the service features etc. Figure 5-8 describes the simplistic approach to carry out PBA analysis.

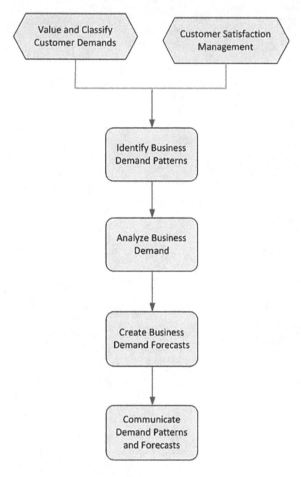

Figure 5-8. *PBA Analysis*

The pattern of business activity for a cloud consumer as described in the examples above would mean the variability of demand for compute resources based on seasonality, days of the month, specific months etc.

Every business goes through seasonal fluctuations. As an example the retailers see increased business activity during the holiday season where the demand increases multifold as customers rush to shop during this period.

New product launches by a consumer company can also generate enormous interest in the website and products of a company. There have been instances where such product launches have resulted in the company's websites getting overwhelmed with traffic and crashing.

The pattern of business activity analysis in cloud environments should provide the following basic information:

- The service catalog items being ordered by the customers

- The frequency and demand pattern of the capacity usage

- The location of the catalogue items

- The utilization at the location level

- Utilization at the catalog item level

The frequency and demand of catalog items at various locations (data centers) provides the basic input for analysis of patterns of business activity. This data is fed into forecasting and analysis tools to generate the capacity required for various services and components. Pattern of business activity for a cloud provider is a complex challenge. The cloud providers used specialized sometimes proprietary analysis tools to gauge the pattern of business activity. For a cloud provider, there may be huge variability in demand because of the nature of business and the cloud provider has to cater to these variations in demand.

This is achieved by a mix of various options to consumers including discounted prices for long term commitment, providing spot instances to customers at cheaper prices to use idle capacity.

For a cloud consumer handling the pattern of business activity becomes easier since now capacity can be provisioned on demand when needed and released during lean periods.

Then forecasting projections, trending and modeling are used to project the PBA to provide details on future patterns of orders and usage of the cloud infrastructure. See later chapters to read more on trending and forecasting.

Service Portfolio: Service portfolio management is the process that manages the service life cycle. These services may include services that are to be launched in the market, live services listed in the service catalog and services that are no longer available. Here the retired services, the pipeline services and the live services in a service portfolio are analyzed and provided as inputs of capacity for cloud computing. These inputs are provided by service portfolio management teams to cloud service providers or the cloud capacity manager and architects. The cloud provider will decide on what services are being offered and what new services are to be offered to customers. The cloud consumer, on the other hand, can select the cloud model for delivering certain services that that are in the pipeline or currently offered.

Service Levels for Availability and Performance: Depending on the desired service levels, the capacity and performance requirements of the cloud computing service may vary. As an example, a higher level of availability commitment will require replication of data and usage of multiple machines or availability of higher level of spare machines. These spare machines can be provisioned in cases of infrastructure downtimes. A higher service performance level will require higher-end resources in terms of compute, storage and network.

The performance data and current performance levels are important indicators for what needs to change in the new service offering or how existing services need to be changed. Regular monitoring of the cloud service provides inputs on pattern of business activity, service levels, availability and capacity and how these impact the capacity management for cloud services. Finally on the basis of all aggregated inputs from above mentioned processes like demand management, service portfolio management, financial management etc, the cloud provider can start designing the capacity of cloud services or the CSP(core service package) prime service like IaaS and SLP (service level package) which contain additional value adds like management, support and maintenance. In later chapters we will closely take a look at procedures for implementing the same.

The cloud consumer can choose the deployment options based on availability and performance requirements. As an example, cloud providers provide options of deploying applications in multiple fault tolerant availability zones and also options of deploying an application across multiple geographies. These options provide higher availability to the applications.

Cloud Service Consumer

The service consumer on the other hand primarily would be focused on reduction of TCO by leveraging the Opex model and the potential benefits of pay per use. The business capacity function for a service consumer will be more inclined toward cost reduction by evaluating the costs associated with various cloud service providers.

Besides this, the service consumer will still need to perform certain functions for capacity planning like business forecasting, financial planning, creating a pattern of business activity analysis, estimating demand, service level negotiations and application and process re-engineering. All these functions help consumers in setting up a best fit approach where cloud computing is concerned. With cloud computing, service consumers can truly look at options the cloud can provide on demand for cost justifiable capacity.

The cloud consumer's capacity planning is impacted because of the cloud model and rather than have an upfront investment in capacity, the capacity is sourced based on a pay per use model in the cloud.

The multiple options available in the cloud and the ever changing prices from cloud providers make calculations of TCO in the cloud model an extensive exercise.

Cloud service consumers, while developing new applications, focus on creating the base case of utilization of an application i.e. the number of users or number of transactions. They can now plan for capacity incrementally as the cloud can work in a scale out model wherein the application can work on multiple machines simultaneously and increase or decrease the number of nodes on which it is working.

In the Software as a Service model the consumer can now source applications on pay per transaction or pay per user per month kind of a model.

This enables the consumer to easily map the business demand to capacity and cost. Since the pay per users model gives you capacity on demand, the same can be linked to the number of users anticipated to avail the service in a particular period based on business demand.

There is no penalty to the cloud consumer if the demand forecast goes wrong as there is no unused capacity being bought in anticipation of demand. Now the procurement is simpler and faster and done when the demand actually arises rather than being done based on a forecast.

The capital expenditure is low since the capacity is not bought upfront. However, the Opex may be higher for which financial planning aspects like cost of capital, return on investment, total cost of ownership etc. are to be applied on the Opex model to compare the various options available from cloud providers/aggregators.

Service Capacity Management in the Cloud

An enterprise may consume multiple types of clouds or cloud services and also retain services within the enterprise to such a level that they still have to estimate service capacity. However, component capacity for on demand components is performed by the cloud provider.

The focus of service capacity management is to identify and understand the cloud services, their use of resources, working patterns, peaks and troughs, to ensure that the services meet their SLA targets, so as to ensure that the services meet the required needs.

In the cloud model, the services that the aggregator provides may come from multiple cloud vendors and thus the cloud aggregator aggregates various services and provides a combined service to the end consumer. Figure 5-9 broadly describes various service components. In cloud based scenario ownership and control these components may vary as described earlier.

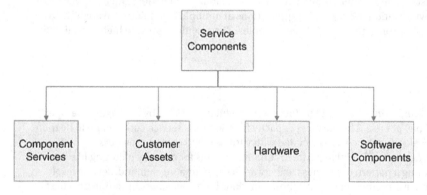

Figure 5-9. Service Components

The customer IT department may instead act as an aggregator by aggregating various services offered by cloud providers. The cloud consumer leverages the IT services provided by the cloud providers and creates higher level services.

As an example, in the infrastructure as a service model the cloud consumer is not concerned with the underlying hardware and virtualization and just consumes it as a service available on the cloud. For instance, it might create a higher level service such as database as a service by providing managed databases on top of the IaaS to its departments or users.

Thus the level at which control and management is exercised in the cloud model is different from the levels at which service capacity may be done in the traditional IT environments.

Figure 5-10 describes the procedure to forecast the service demand. Though this is purely demand management function but inputs from service capacity are used to demand calculations and demand forecasts are fed into capacity management process.

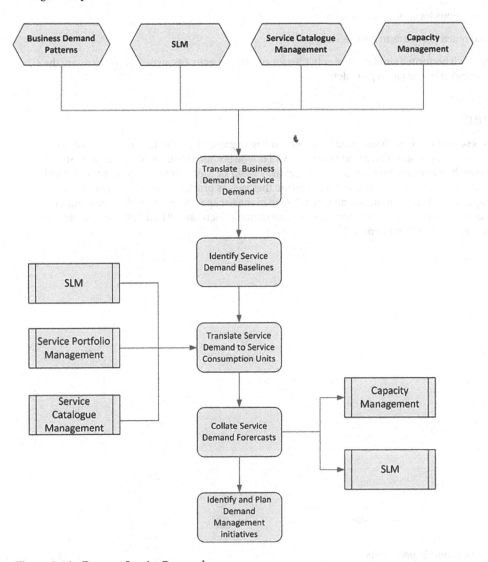

Figure 5-10. *Forecast Service Demands*

Cloud Service Provider

The service provided by the cloud provider can be any of the flavors (IaaS, PaaS, SaaS) and the cloud provider has to ensure that the capacity of services is available for use by the cloud consumers. The cloud provider measures the following key parameters to keep tabs on the capacity of the cloud service being offered and takes appropriate actions to ensure the service level agreements (or SLAs) are maintained and the services are available to service consumers:

- Data collection and thresholds

- Analysis of the current and future usage of the services

- Roll ups of individual components which constitute the cloud service

- Monitoring of SLAs

- Workloads at various locations/datacenters

- Proactive and reactive actions to enhance capacity.

The cloud aggregator will perform a similar set of activities for service capacity because their services are the aggregation of services provided by the cloud providers.

Cloud Consumer

The cloud consumer uses services from various cloud providers and aggregators and bundles these services to provide applications and utilities to users. The cloud consumer will not be bothered with how the service capacity of these cloud providers will be managed. Instead, they will primarily monitor the SLAs of the cloud provider and aggregators. They will also ensure that any services which they are themselves providing on top of the cloud are monitored for service capacity and appropriate actions are taken to manage capacity in a cost effective manner.

Figure 5-11 describes the increase in cost as service usage and demand increases. P1 and P2 is the service price. S1, S2 and D1, D2 being service supply and demand.

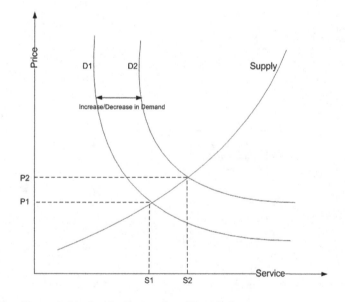

Figure 5-11. *Service Demand and Supply Curve*

The IT services can be monitored through various monitoring approaches and tools which use simulated transactions or sniffing the data on the network to monitor the end user's view of the services. Besides this there are several toolsets available that capture end users' service experience and creates customer satisfaction reports. For example Figure 5-12 shows the usage and end user experience of a user using Microsoft Outlook application. This dashboard provides an integrated view of all the problems, various desktop usage metrics, and outlier application performance measurements associated with the Outlook application.

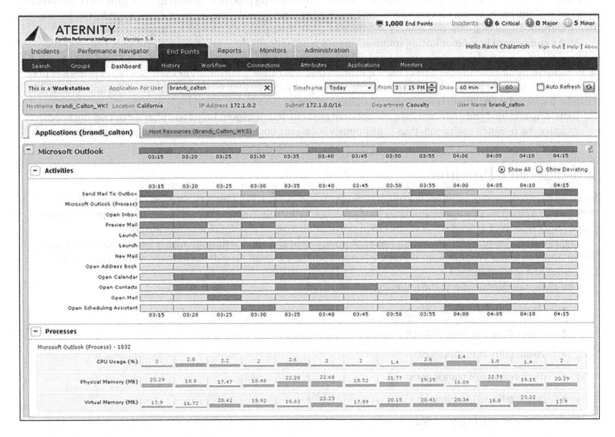

Figure 5-12. *Aternity's Performance Intelligence*

In this current age of increasing complexity and the highly distributed nature of virtualized environments, cloud computing, virtual desktops, and web 2.0 applications, there is a strong need to capture, review and improve the end user experience. There are various application/service performance management technologies that monitor the three prime user experience components like application/service performance, infrastructure performance and user productivity. These toolsets use real-time aggregation, analysis and correlation of all these metrics and showcase the results in dashboards.

As an example, the network connectivity to the cloud service may be the responsibility of the cloud consumer. And this has to be monitored for usage and bandwidth along with the application of above mentioned techniques so that the cloud consumer can identify the problems and increase the network bandwidth to access applications/resources available on the cloud.

Component Capacity Management in the Cloud

The focus of component capacity management is to identify and understand the resource requirements, performance levels, and utilization trends of each of the individual components within the cloud environment. These components like servers, security components, network components, storage, software when aggregated from a service like email. The performance data from components is recorded, analyzed, and reported for resource planning and component capacity management. Automated threshold management and alerting mechanism help in managing all components, to ensure that situations where service targets are breached or threatened by component usage or performance are rapidly identified, and cost-effective actions to reduce or avoid their potential impact are implemented.

At the component layer, monitoring solutions should automatically determine normal end-user response time and send alerts to warn of potential service level failures, improving the cloud provider's ability to find the root cause for an incident by pinpointing the part of the application that was causing the fault. For example, cloud providers may use monitoring tools for performance management and impact analysis to determine the parts of the application that would be impacted even if there is a change in database schema.

Gathering and analyzing relevant data, component capacity management helps you plan for upcoming needs and optimize the resource utilization, thus continuously balancing cost against capacity and supply against demand.

Cloud Service Provider

The cloud service provider monitors the underlying components like CPU, Memory, Storage, OS, etc. of a cloud service while a cloud service aggregator or a cloud customer will be monitoring the service levels and performance related requirements of a cloud service. The cloud provider also needs this data for billing purposes.

The cloud service provider has to monitor each component and service through highly automated tools and uses automation to auto-tune or auto-correct. It is impossible for a cloud provider to manage without automated monitoring and resolution tools.

The cloud provider monitors the following:

- Availability of each service

- Performance of each service

- Availability of components

- Performance of components

- Availability of integrations

- Performance of integrations

The monitoring is done from inside the data centers and also from outside locations to monitor the performance impact or unavailability due to network issues from other locations.

Cloud Consumer

The cloud consumer will also monitor the resource/component capacity to make decisions on capacity expansion and also to make decisions to scale out the infrastructure.

An example of this would be the monitoring of a server for CPU and RAM. In case the server reaches capacity, the cloud consumer can configure automation to spin new machines which start taking the workload.

Some cloud providers provide basic component monitoring data to the cloud consumers to enable them to use resource utilization and performance reports to decide on resource expansion actions and performance tuning of applications.

Now let us deep dive into sub processes or procedures of capacity management that are specific to cloud environments. These procedures can be broadly categorized into:

- **Capacity calculation for new services**

- **Ongoing capacity management**

Figure 5-13 showcases the cloud capacity management process. In rest of the chapters we will deep dive into each procedure area.

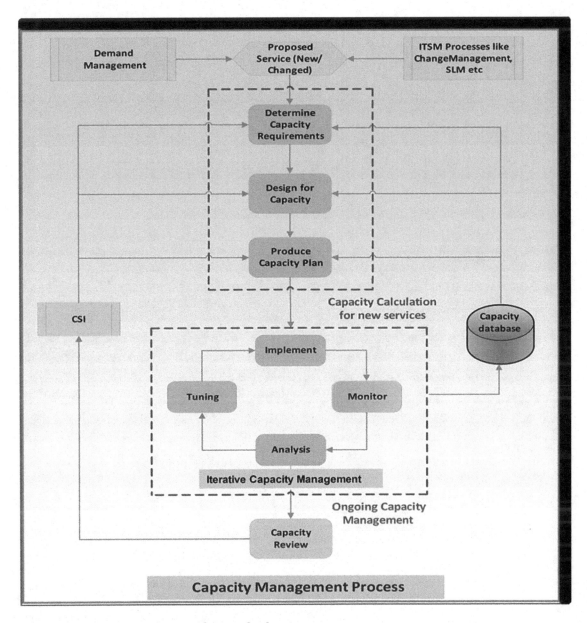

Figure 5-13. *Capacity management focus in cloud environment*

■ ■ ■

CHAPTER 6

Capacity Planning

After gaining an understanding of the concepts of cloud computing and capacity management in prior chapters, this chapter focuses on capacity management as a process in the cloud. This chapter explains a pragmatic approach for implementing best practices in cloud capacity management that will help cloud service providers in designing and implementing capacity management processes in the most cost-effective fashion. Capacity management as a process has been described in Chapters 4 and 5, and should be adopted to ensure optimum utilization of capacity for cloud providers and consumers alike. The conventional IT service model may not be the best fit for the cloud environment. This chapter bridges the gap between traditional capacity management practices and cloud service models, and it showcases capacity management process design and implementation in the cloud landscape using IT service management best practices. Capacity management from the cloud service provider's view has been segregated into *capacity management for new services* and *ongoing capacity management* for existing services. This chapter will present an integrated scenario of how ITSM best practices for capacity planning get addressed in the cloud environment.

Capacity Planning

In any cloud deployment model, either private or public cloud, capacity management basic principles will remain the same and will continue to serve the prime goal of achieving cost justifiable capacity to meet the current and future needs of the business.

Critical success factors for determining capacity for services remain the input data (service levels, current usage, and future demand) from which a capacity plan will be made. Remember, a capacity plan is the outcome of the capacity planning process.

For efficient capacity planning, it is important to categorize the service into measurable units. Workloads may be analyzed for determining service levels requirements. Current capacity levels must be measured so that forecasts can be made based on the gap between current and expected capacity.

Inputs from management for capacity planning may include the following:

- Expected growth in the business

- Requirements for implementing new applications

- Planned acquisitions or divestitures

- Financial plans

- Requests for consolidation of IT resources

Capacity planning is the key area around which concepts like resource utilization and cost justifiable capacity are based. In this book, we will approach capacity planning from the service provider's perspective. In any IT-driven business service first inputs for planning capacity will come from demand for that service and the corresponding data may come from the demand management process.

The demand management process may use market research tools and other techniques for anticipating demand for a particular IT service. This demand data is fed into capacity management procedures to come up with a capacity plan to fulfill future demand. Another input for planning capacity may come from usage profiles of services. Usage of an IT service can be captured from the component or resource layer, which in the cloud environment may include usage of virtual CPUs, storage, network, and other associated components.

When done effectively, capacity planning ensures a reduction in resource waste and optimized resource utilization. In modern data centers, underutilized or idle machines keep consuming power and depreciate day by day. Capacity planning is an attempt to resolve these issues by planning and optimizing the data center environment to handle what the business needs, and it provides room for spikes and expansion without wasting resources.

We will delve into this in later sections to see how capacity planning is positioned in the overall capacity management process.

For a cloud provider, it is essential to maximize the utilization of available capacity as well as plan for future demand for capacity.

The difference for a cloud provider comes in the shape of supply and pricing. Thus, the lever of pricing and supply plays in important role in cloud capacity planning for the cloud provider, which was never the case with enterprises since they never built capacity to be sold. The cloud provider can lower pricing and create innovative offerings to increase the consumption of cloud resources.

As an example, a cloud provider may have offerings for consumers wherein capacity can be reserved for a period, so the cloud provider has less risk of capacity not getting consumed or lying idle and can thus plan better to service customer needs. The reserved capacity is offered at a lesser hourly rate with an upfront payment to book the capacity in advance.

Other innovative offerings such as spot pricing, wherein available capacity is auctioned in an open market auctioning format online and made available to the highest bidder, also help the cloud provider in utilizing idle resources to the maximum while at the same time providing an option to the cloud consumer to consume the compute resources at a lower price. Thus, variable workloads, which can wait for a lower price, can make use of the spot pricing. Examples of such workloads can be scientific applications and data crunching jobs, which do not provide real-time results.

Capacity Management in the Cloud

Capacity management is considered to be a service design process when a new service is launched or an existing service is modified. After formulation of the service strategy, which considers service demand, the current service portfolio, and IT-related financial planning, the service is designed in concert with the required service features, service levels, change management processes, customers' ever-changing business needs, etc. Capacity planning is tuned according to these business requirements. Thus, correctly designing service capacity becomes a critical success factor for IT services rollout and its business alignment.

In a cloud environment, the capacity management process is the key differentiator for ensuring success in running business processes. There are situations wherein the ease of server or infrastructure deployment is mistaken for cheap infrastructure deployment. Ease of deployment without governance and control mechanisms in place can result in *virtual sprawl*. Virtual machine sprawl is the result of over-capacity allocation and is one of the pain areas wherein enterprises fail to leverage the true benefits of the cloud model. Capacity planning aims at providing mitigation to such situations by making sure optimum levels of capacity are in place.

In the cloud model, ordering compute capacity is made simpler and faster. However, this may result in unused machines being procured and lying idle. It is essential that appropriate controls are in place to find and eliminate VM sprawl so that people or departments do not buy compute capacity when it is not needed and that compute capacity is released back when not needed.

Figure 6-1 displays the process to manage VM sprawl through a resource reclamation framework. These processes get initiated by identification of workload efficiencies, validation of the same, reclaiming the identified underutilized resources, and monitoring the environment for further resource and cost optimization. Without reporting and control processes to control the above, it is possible for customers in cloud environments to lose money because of unused but procured compute capacity.

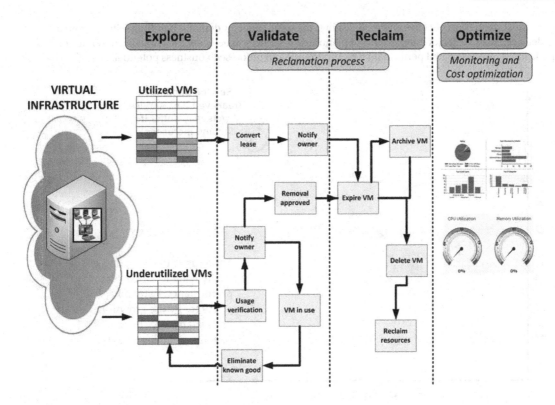

Figure 6-1. *Resource reclamation process*

In a cloud environment, the capacity management process will also be focused on a detailed understanding of the component-level side of the business (all of the underlying virtual infrastructure such as servers, network bandwidth, storage, and load balancers). To achieve the desired benefits of a cloud implementation, the process will need to cover all aspects of the service and the underlying infrastructure, application performance monitoring, workload placements, and so on.

Enterprises leveraging cloud solutions or planning to move on to cloud models must rethink their capacity allocation strategy by focusing on application performance awareness and integrating with the management stack. A cloud solution must offer the following:

- An end-to-end view of infrastructure resources

- A forward-looking view on capacity consumption using modeling and simulation techniques

- Proactive capacity allocation

- The capability to define technical, business, and compliance rules for workload placement

Besides adapting to the new capacity management strategy, enterprises also have to choose and implement the required capacity management toolsets. These toolsets not only monitor IT infrastructure, but application behavior as well.

An enterprise then seeks applications and data that facilitate business processes and run those processes and store critical data. Hardware capacity plays an important role. Businesses, by their nature, seek growth, and this must be supported by infrastructure performance to facilitate those ever-growing business applications. Capacity must be able to intelligently tune itself according to criticalities that may arise due to business dynamics, seasons, and sudden peaks—and yet must still be cost effective. Figure 6-2 shows the basic capacity-demand handling scheme from a service provider's perspective. Major components in planning for service capacity are the criticality of service or business applications, the associated performance requirements, and unforeseen business potential.

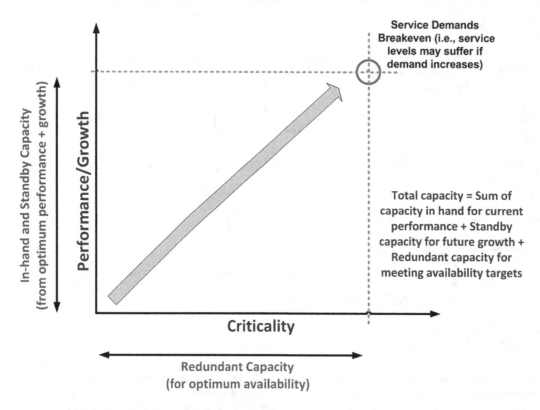

Figure 6-2. *Capacity management meeting demand*

On the basis of these parameters, capacity planning needs to be tuned. Various capacity definitions that can be considered may be *capacity in use*, which is used for supporting the existing service levels, and *standby capacity,* which is required to fulfill the capacity-related needs of immediate peaks and troughs, and also for any failures that may occur in the capacity in use. *Redundant capacity* can be thought of as overall capacity inventory, which is maintained as per business continuity planning, service demand, service portfolio management, and other long term inputs for strategic capacity planning purposes. Redundant capacity always acts as a cushion for standby capacity requirements. The redundant capacity is what is available for future expansion of the current workloads. For a cloud service provider, overall capacity management and planning will revolve around seeking the optimum balance around these components—with total capacity to provide a cloud service being the sum of all components: capacity in use, standby capacity, and redundant capacity.

Business criticality, the importance of services to the business, must be interpreted well in order to see the unforeseen events leading to service outages; proactive measures like redundancy, backup, recovery, and failover must stand firm against any downtime challenge. Capacity management procedures must be able to clearly formulate uptime requirements in terms of data center tiers organized by business criticality, performance requirements, and the growth plan. Besides this, capacity management procedures must keep an eye on demand and business growth plans to ensure that demand is met by standby capacity and is able to support continued service levels.

Total service requirements can be driven from performance requirements, future growth needs, and business criticality of the service.

Performance Requirements

Performance requirements may include current capacity requirements like CPUs, network connections, I/O channels, etc. that an application may need to perform at the desired level and to meet user expectations. This can be gathered from the original configuration requirements from application deployment, performance testing, and application performance monitoring.

In a cloud model, some cloud providers may provide guaranteed performance on storage IOPS. These features can be used to provide guaranteed performance for applications. Performance requirements of a workload may determine the choice of a cloud provider based on the performance guarantee or based on the architecture of a particular cloud service.

Business Criticality

Business criticality specifies the importance of the application or the service to the business. An application can be either a mainstream application running the business or a business-supporting application like e-mail. Any impact on the application can have substantial business impact as well. Business criticality information can be gathered from a business impact analysis and/or a disaster recovery plan.

The business criticality is a key decision point in migration to a client environment and the type of cloud provider the enterprise may select. Service levels offered by the cloud provider and the underlying architecture of a public cloud may be key decision points for cloud migration.

An enterprise may decide to keep the business critical applications in an in-house, private cloud to support the availability and performance needs of such applications.

Future Growth

This specifies the expected growth in demand of the service and over a given period of, say, the next three years. Information is provided from forecasting plans based on historical utilization and upcoming business plans like market expansion and other factors.

A capacity management approach for cloud service providers must ensure that customer's business needs are supported by optimum capacity at all layers in a cost-effective way. Cloud service providers must provide two options of capacity solutions.

The first option may begin with planning from scratch using past experience, analysis of the current datacenter space, demand data, analysis of the customer's capacity requirements, assured service levels, availability and performance needs of services, etc. This is done when a new business service is at hand and the service provider has to start right from the beginning (i.e., planning for datacenter space, chassis, cooling and power requirements, hardware, software and other tools and technologies including virtualization). These are prerequisites for architecting and planning for capacity whenever a new service is in consideration.

The other option is capacity management for existing service in which performance monitoring plays the vital role. Along with this, performance analysis carried out to maintain the performance levels and seek continual service improvement actions through threshold management and tuning.

Hence, we can summarize capacity management goals in a cloud environment as the following:

- Reduction of waste of resources
- Efficient resource utilization
- Support service-level monitoring and management
- Workload management
- Forecasting infrastructure growth
- Controlling VM sprawl
- Automatic allocation of resources in failures
- Handling unforeseen and seasonal demands effectively
- Ensuring cloud economies in multi-cloud environments like public clouds and hybrid clouds

■ ■ ■

CHAPTER 7

Determining Capacity Requirements for New Services

After defining capacity management and looking at various key aspects on capacity management in Chapter 6, this chapter explains how capacity management is performed for new services and what capacity requirements must be gathered for subsequent capacity design. Various procedures have been defined, enabling service providers to determine capacity requirements for new services. These procedures include gathering capacity requirements through demand anticipation, identification of vital business functions, understanding cost implications, gathering performance related requirements, etc. Emphasis has been given on specifying multi-vendor service level agreements (SLAs), operational level agreements (OLAs), and Underpinning Contracts (UCs) so that capacity requirements are met as specified. These requirements, once gathered, form the building blocks for capacity design.

Capacity Calculation for New Services

Capacity management is involved in the design of new or changing services and makes recommendations for the procurement of cloud infrastructure, where capacity and/or performance are factors. These decisions are facilitated by scaling algorithms and capacity planning. Demand management also plays a vital role in figuring out unforeseen infrastructure capacity requirements by understanding the usage patterns formally known as Patterns of Business Activities (PBA). Demand information should further drill down to the service-wise component level infrastructure elements like CPU, memory, network, and storage to ensure that sufficient capacity design and provisioning exists to support future business processes.

Determine Capacity Requirements

The procedures for determining capacity requirements are as follows:

- Understand capacity requirements and vital business functions
- Capacity demand coupling
- Provide the cost of capacity inputs
- Specify performance targets

Figure 7-1 describes the procedures and activities that must be carried out to gather capacity requirements that are perfectly aligned to the business. Other ITSM processes like demand management, service level management, change management, and financial management provide the required information for capacity requirement gathering.

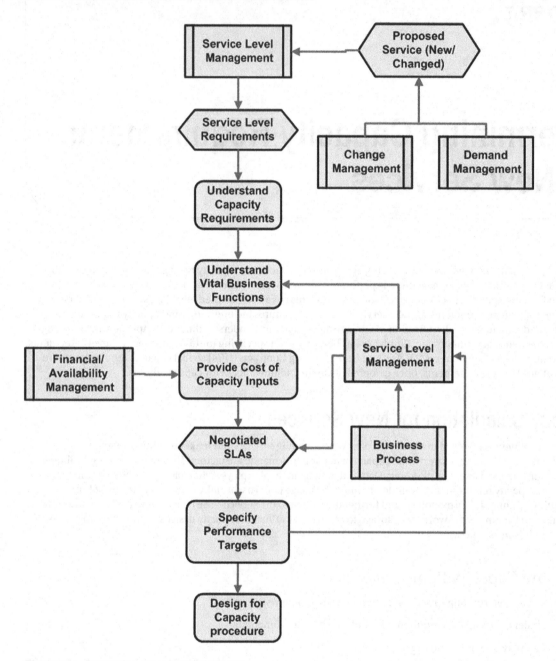

Figure 7-1. *Determine capacity requirements*

These requirements must be well understood and—more importantly—well interpreted by capacity management processes.

Understand Capacity Requirements and Vital Business Functions

This is the information that is primarily utilized for IT capacity, service availability, and IT service continuity. Business-critical elements of business processes supported by IT services are understood by capacity management for special consideration in design requirements supporting desired performance. For example, a client may opt for any of the cloud deployment models as per their business requirements.

A business and financial services (BFS) customer may want to keep core staff and applications on a private cloud and other third party and contractual staff on a public cloud, including services like e-mail and messaging. Capacity planning must be able to formulate and address those business needs efficiently and effectively.

For any new business service, the service provider must dive into understanding and deciding on appropriate service levels. Service levels must be then mapped with applications and infrastructural requirements. Various business cases must be prepared in order to get a long term capacity view. Various capacity parameters like capacity in use, standby capacity, and redundant capacity must be considered to gather all possible capacity requirements for all vital business functions. On the basis of capacity and redundancy requirements for supporting the business processes, capacity management must ensure that all capacity components like tier-wise data center configuration, space, hardware, and tools are in place to serve business application criticality and performance needs.

On the basis of vital business functions, the cloud service provider may think of providing required capacity to accommodate different data center tiers (i.e., Tier 1, 2, 3, or 4). The tier levels increment as the availability increases and decrease in line with estimated downtime hours. Tier ratings of data centers may help providers in planning for business capacity and performance needs. These data center tiers can be classified as follows:

- Tier 1: Basic site infrastructure with non-redundant capacity components

- Tier 2: Redundant site infrastructure capacity components

- Tier 3: Concurrently maintainable site infrastructure

- Tier 4: Fault tolerant site infrastructure

Basic data center standards and configuration references must be kept in mind when deciding on data center tiers. For example, a data center (DC) component configuration mix of Tier 2 and 3 would result in a Tier 2 DC configuration standard. Besides this, the capacity approach for the data center may consider other parameters, such as DC space and layout, cabling standards, power, cooling, tiers as discussed here, and other environmental and regulatory considerations.

Capacity requirements at all levels (i.e., business, service, and component) must be discussed and agreed upon, and formal sign off must be given. Performance criteria in terms of capacity (physical and virtual servers, databases, middleware, storage, networks, facilities, etc.) and derived service levels from business and users of IT should be understood and translated in terms of utilization rates.,

As depicted in Figure 7-2, the redundant capacity needs to be planned to cater to growth predictions. If the redundant capacity is not planned, the IT service may not be able to render services because of lack of capacity.

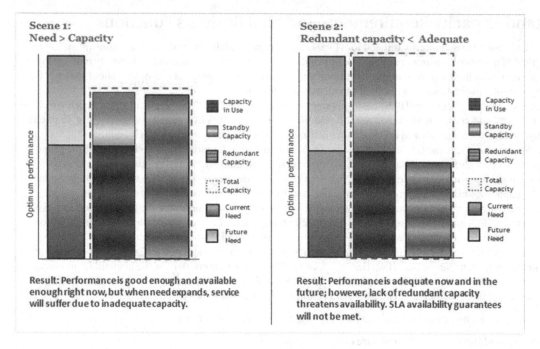

Figure 7-2. *Capacity requirements and vital business functions*

Cloud computing provides a way out since enterprises don't need to keep redundant capacity but can procure capacity on demand from a cloud provider. However, from a cloud provider's perspective, redundant capacity has to be available for servicing variable workloads and variable demand from customers.

Hence, total capacity requirements are an aggregation of meeting current performance goals, future need, and availability/recovery goals of all applications and services. Future need is covered by standby capacity above what is currently being used.

Availability/recovery is typically enabled through redundancy. This redundancy can be any of the following:

- Component redundancy

- Full resource redundancy (redundant servers, storage arrays, switches, UPS (uninterruptible power supply), cooling)

- Data redundancy (data snapshots, mirrors, backup copies)

If demand exceeds capacity available for planned growth and/or does not leave enough redundant capacity, service levels will be compromised. Either additional physical capacity will need to be added or another workload will need to be removed from the pool of available capacity.

Understanding Disaster Recovery Requirements for Capacity

It is also essential to take into consideration the disaster recovery (DR) requirements while planning for capacity. The DR site will need capacity to ensure that in the case of a failure, the critical systems marked for being moved to the DR site are capable of performing as defined in the SLAs.

The DR site can be passive and only brought up in case of a disaster being declared on the primary site. Alternatively, the DR site can be an active site. In this case, the DR site has active instances running and in use, and the two sites are used as a failover for each other. Capacity planning should provide for monitoring and management of capacity at the DR site in a similar fashion to that for the primary site.

The cloud provider may provide multiple data centers and options to customers to leverage multiple datacenters to provide disaster recovery capabilities to customers. The customers having a private cloud or a traditional deployment in house can leverage the cloud provider for disaster recovery.

Capacity Demand Coupling

Capacity for services must be based on demand forecasts and patterns of business activity. Capacity is controlled by demand. That is, the consumption cycle consumes demand and the production cycle produces demand (see Figure 7-3).

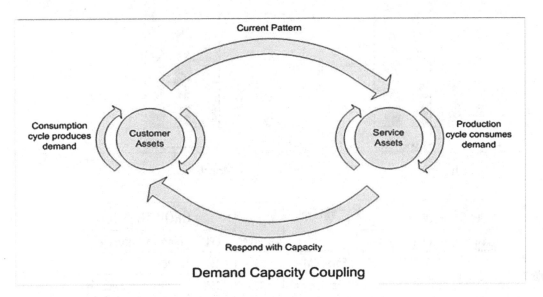

Figure 7-3. *Capacity and demand*

The consumption cycle produces demand for more resources. As an example, an increase in users of an e-mail service will result in increased demand for capacity, which is consumed by the production cycle. Thus, the demand from customers or users drives the capacity demand from the back-end production cycle to cater to that demand.

In a cloud provider scenario, the demand comes from the users of cloud services. In an enterprise environment, the enterprises can leverage the on-demand provisioning of resources to service the demand capacity coupling better with increased agility. The demand management process provides inputs to the Pattern of Business Activities (PBAs) to help cloud providers to better understand capacity-related requirements to meet future service demand effectively. This demand pattern may be formulated in terms of need for cloud infrastructure to be added over a period of time. A pattern of business activities analysis must be done by people managing demand and capacity collectively. Information like key performance indicators (KPIs), CSAT scores, and customer surveys can be used for carrying out this analysis. Business capacity planning may begin here on the basis of PBA analysis, business activity modeling, forecasts, and demand data. These patterns are codified, and user profiles are created. There are various toolsets with built-in algorithms and statistical methods to carry out such analysis. Demand management inputs must be able to help capacity planners to proactively anticipate capacity usage associated with the service. This will ensure that a balance between standby and current capacity is maintained and service levels are supported by capacity management without any unwanted surprises.

Figure 7-4 provides a sample that includes the forecast of new VMs with a mix of different types of virtual machines. This forecast is then used by the capacity planning processes to plan for capacity addition and the timelines when this new capacity needs to be added.

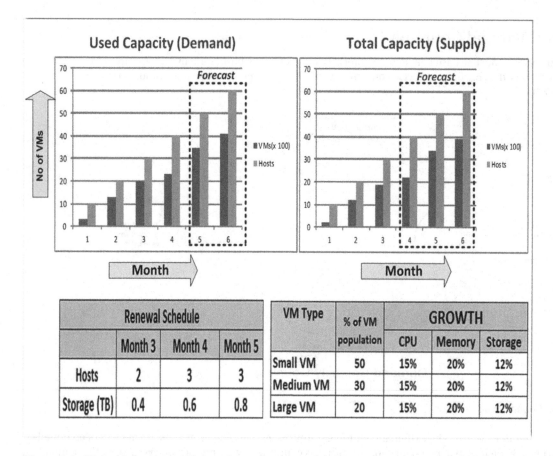

Figure 7-4. *Virtual infrastructure forecasting and resource planning*

In a particular company, usage on an order-processing application goes up 40 percent on the second and fourth Friday of each month. These usage spikes are normal and recurring, and the underlying IT infrastructure can handle them without degradation, so IT does not have to respond to their occurrence. By understanding that this is a normal change, IT can set a baseline indicating that all fluctuations within a certain range are normal and do not require action. That's difficult to do, however, because of the complexity of the underlying IT infrastructure and usage patterns in the modern data center. Complicating the situation is the fact that the rhythms themselves may change over time. The company introduced a new product line that placed an additional burden on the order-processing application. This causes a 60 percent increase in workload on the second and fourth Friday of each month. This 60 percent increase now represents the new normal peak for that application. Enterprises struggle to monitor and forecast the average and peak demand for services; not surprisingly, decision making based on forecasts can go wrong. The cloud computing model can make things simpler for an enterprise wherein they can buy capacity on demand from a cloud provider in case of increased capacity. A hybrid cloud model approach where the required capacity is available within the company's datacenter with a burst option to a public cloud for increased workloads is an option that can provide enterprises with cost benefits.

Demand Monitoring

Monitoring demand is about understanding how well you currently support your user's demands for capacity. Monitoring capacity demand levels can tell you how many users require resources and how many resources each business activity consumes. It also provides valuable information on the current capacity levels of resources so that IT will know how to support new services as they are introduced into the environment, as well as how new services will affect current SLAs. In this case, it is essential to understand the effective capacity of a resource.

When the future forecast demand for capacity is addressed through Capex in anticipation of future demand, the provider's capacity increases, and there is overcapacity for the time period when demand picks up but is not yet consuming all the capacity provisioned. The demand catches up with the capacity available in a rising demand scenario and will result in under capacity. In a falling demand scenario, there will be overcapacity.

The trick is in balancing the demand and supply through price changes and other efforts including new services and new geographies to take care of a falling demand scenario. The ability of the cloud provider to anticipate the rise and fall in demand is the key to being a successful cloud provider.

In the case of under capacity, the cloud consumers may not be able to provision resources or the performance SLAs will suffer, which will result in customer dissatisfaction and financial loss because of the lost opportunity to sell additional capacity.

Thus, the balance between available capacity, standby capacity, and redundant capacity has to be fine-tuned through advanced analytics and tools.

Providing Cost of Capacity Inputs

In conjunction with financial budgets and plans, capacity management must provide for the cost of fulfilling specified service level requests. This forms the basis of the SLA negotiation between the cloud service provider (creator/aggregator) and the customer. This can be an iterative activity until the SLAs are negotiated. For any cloud where resources can be deployed in a self-service fashion, cost models, metering, and chargeback procedures for resources should be in place. There are several key features when implementing chargebacks. Chargebacks and showbacks should be based on either allocated or actual resource usage. An allocation-based cost model will charge customers on duration-based usage, and a usage-based model will charge customers on an actual usage basis. Licensing, power, data center type and space, and other expenses related to a customer's allocation must be factored in to reflect the total cost that each tenant incurs. Chargeback reporting needs to be integrated into a financial system or other budgetary system

Thus the cost of the service is based on individual components of the service (such as the facilities cost, network cost, virtual server cost, and virtual storage cost). The cloud provider typically provides a unified bill and can drill down to individual cost components (see Figure 7-5).

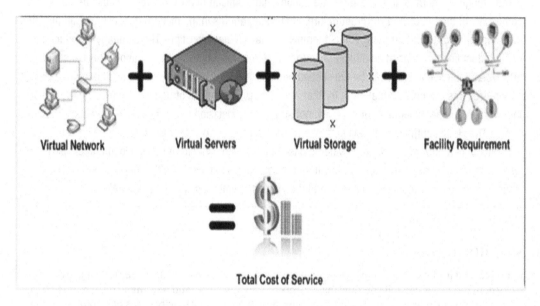

Figure 7-5. *Costs of capacity inputs*

The cloud consumer can base the decisions of cloud procurement on the overall bill as well as the individual components provided by the cloud provider. As an example, if the network usage of an application is extremely high, the cloud consumer may decide to consume it from an in-premise data center rather than a cloud provider.

Specifying Performance Targets

Negotiated SLAs are translated into specific performance targets that are to be supported by management. This forms the basis of negotiation of OLAs and UCs for the fulfillment of SLAs. A SLA between the cloud service provider and the customer should do the following:

- Define what service will be provided.

- Establish the manner in which (how) service will be provided.

- Establish the quality standard to be achieved.

- Establish measurement criteria.

- Establish reporting criteria.

- Establish cost of delivery.

In a multi-provider environment, the complexity of SLAs increases. Since each provider is providing only parts of a service, the SLAs, OLAs, and UCs need to be created to cover the complex scenarios.

Measurement tools for calculation of service levels are needed to compute such complex service level scenarios. Monitoring needs to be in place to determine where the service has failed so that appropriate service levels are appropriately computed.

Cloud Service Provider

SLAs with a service provider will be mostly standardized as their service levels and availability targets are standardized. The service provider at times may customize their SLAs based on service volumes provided to service aggregators or consumers. SLA management for a service provider is a relatively simple task as compared with a cloud service aggregator. The service provider also may have OLAs within the organization.

Cloud Service Aggregator

Service level management for a service aggregator is a cumbersome process because of the involvement of all types of agreements, like SLAs with customers and OLAs within organizational entities. All these SLAs and multi-vendor environments contribute to the customer SLA. The cloud service aggregator also may need to be involved in managing UCs with other service creators.

Consumer

SLAs between cloud service providers and customers must primarily take into account the customer's business needs and services that support them. When a cloud service provider ensures that application requirements can be served as required, negotiation on SLA clauses, penalties, dispute policies, etc. must be established.

For the cloud consumer, the challenge is that the cloud providers and cloud aggregators have published SLAs and those are fixed. The consumer doesn't have the flexibility to fine-tune or change the SLAs as per their requirements since they are buying a standardized service from the cloud provider or aggregator.

The cloud consumer will have to take into account the complexity and a way to monitor the SLA of the cloud provider to provide the necessary services to the internal organization and keep track of penalties and service charges.

Figure 7-6 depicts the agreements that exist in cloud delivery chain. In a cloud value chain, there is underpinning, a UP service agreement relationship between cloud services aggregator and service creators, operational level agreements, OLAs, within the aggregator's organization and service level agreement, and SLAs with customers.

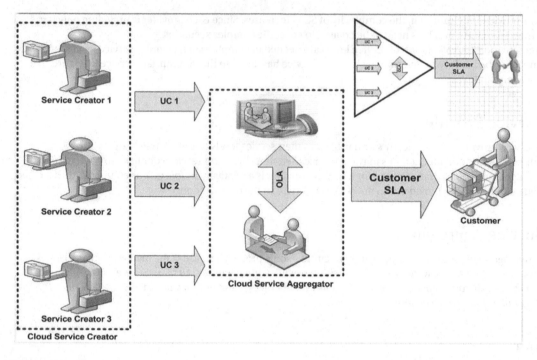

Figure 7-6. *Cloud service agreements*

The providers are bound by contract to provide a certain level of services. Many services specified in their contract have direct or indirect impact on the actions of other participants in the service delivery chain. If those actions are not adequately managed, then a service provider could be at risk of being in default on the service level and thus the contract.

The essential point of capacity management in virtual environments is to get a handle on performance trends. Understanding the growth rate of a particular component and what will happen if trends continue is vital. In addition, by tracking historical values, a cloud provider can determine the root cause more precisely in case of an incident.

CHAPTER 8

■ ■ ■

Capacity Management Design

This section elaborates on how capacity management is designed in accordance with gathered capacity requirements. Emphasis has been given on how to select the right capacity approach by choosing the best workload placement mechanism infrastructure, defining capacity management architecture and components, and cost optimization measures. This ensures maximum resource utilization and optimum performance in a cost-justifiable manner. One of the key success factors in capacity management is establishing overall capacity architecture. This chapter describes the architecture in various layers that fulfill business- and performance-related requirements from a capacity management perspective. It is essential for any new service that designs for capacity to also take into account service level management, security requirements, availability requirements, application scalability requirements, etc.

Design for Capacity

The procedures for designing capacity are to

- Establish a capacity approach.
- Establish the architecture.
- Apply capacity techniques.
- Establish components and check for cost optimization.

This procedure for capacity management (shown in Figure 8-1) gets triggered once capacity requirements are gathered. Once the capacity requirements have been gathered, the overall capacity management approach for capacity planning and management is established. This may include designing capacity management architecture and models. Capacity techniques are used to establish capacity components, or layers, such as the data, analysis, and presentation layers. Let's take a deep dive into capacity design procedures.

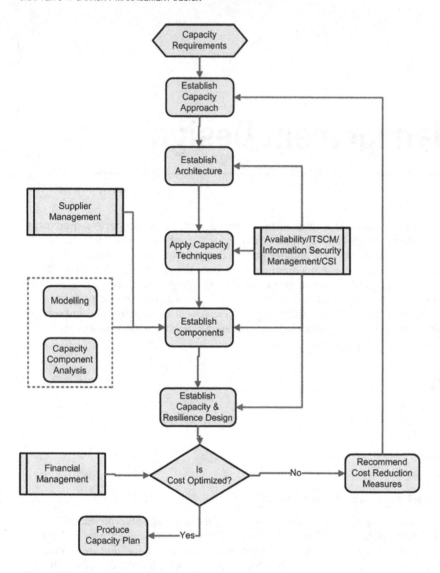

Figure 8-1. *Capacity management design activities*

Establishing Capacity Approach

A capacity approach must ensure maximum cloud infrastructure utilization by hosting the client instances as efficiently as possible. In virtual environments where provisioning of infrastructure is easy, there can be issues of under-provisioning and over-provisioning. So there is a need for an efficient capacity approach that can find a balance between these two.

A capacity approach must be primarily focused on placement of workloads and resource allocation. Fragmented capacity may lead to inefficiencies and may even double the infrastructure required to host the workloads. Capacity procedures must be defined to ensure intelligent allocation of virtual machines as required by the applications.

Capacity management toolsets can be considered to enable the service provider to define technical, business, and compliance rules for workload placement. These workload placement rules are configured in cloud lifecycle management toolsets in the management layer. Rule engines must be evaluated to guarantee the health and accuracy of the capacity management solution.

As shown in Figure 8-2, the best approach for placing workloads or virtual machines on a virtual infrastructure must be used to ensure existing resources are consumed efficiently. As shown in Allocation A, unused patches potentially signify unused capacity, and this would lead to inefficiencies. On the other hand, Allocation B ensures the best possible usage of resources.

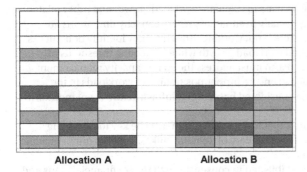

Figure 8-2. *Workload allocation*

A workload is a logical classification of work performed in a virtual infrastructure. Workloads may be classified by who is doing work, what work is being done, and how the work is being done. For example, a service provider must be able to classify the workloads according to business functions like sales, marketing, or finance. Business-relevant workloads are also useful when it comes time to plan for the future.

Business applications must be analyzed for infrastructure usage requirements. There can be two business applications that are equally critical to business but consume resources variably. Capacity management must be able to establish such needs and accordingly classify the service levels associated with applications so that the infrastructure is provided accordingly (such as disk space, compute capacity, memory, and network bandwidth requirements). These measures will help in planning of future system requirements.

Figure 8-3 depicts how planning for workloads is critical for efficient resource utilization. Techniques like estimation, modeling, and load testing can be used for efficient workload planning. Workload Plan A, when placed in the infrastructure, is definitely not the best workload pattern for the available infrastructure whereas Workload Plan B is fit for the available infrastructure, leading to efficiencies and apt resource utilization schemas. There are several toolsets available that specialize in workload planning to help capacity planners in establishing the best approach for capacity.

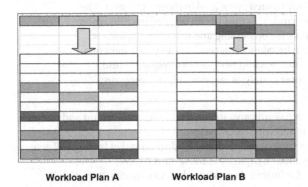

Figure 8-3. *Workload planning*

Based on performance, service level targets, and business vital functions, a high-level approach toward meeting the targets is chosen. For example, a stiff cost focus in performance targets would call for a just-in-time solution, whereas service continuity at stiff performance targets might require solutions to utilize the availability of margin capacity. An approach must be decided upon to provide real-time and historical workload reports that can be used for on-the-fly resource optimization and problem diagnosis. Real-time workload reports must identify under- or over-utilized server capacity, which can be used to optimize the distribution of the workload across all available hardware, as well as to help prevent unnecessary hardware purchases.

While setting up the approach for capacity, service providers must assess the workloads through discovery and inventory of IT assets because these are the prime causes behind capacity bottlenecks. This must be done function-, location-, and environment-wise. Statistical algorithms must be used to calculate workload growth and other related metrics. These reports can also help to diagnose problems, especially in situations where capacity limitations go unnoticed or where load balancing within server farms or clusters is not working properly. They identify bottlenecks and required additional capacity to support expected or desired workload growth while respecting thresholds of resource utilization and response times. The capacity approach also must address the spare capacity management and ensure defragmentation and other techniques are in place to ensure proper positioning of workloads in the infrastructure. Proactive capacity allocation methods must be considered based upon infrastructure event monitoring and analytics.

Whitespace management is the management of the spare capacity in an environment. The key to managing whitespace is analytics that determine optimum spare capacity to take care of demand spikes. Toolsets must calculate the trade-off between cloud capacity and the associated costs.

Besides finalizing these issues, the capacity approach is established in consensus with the set financial plans and budgets. Financial management will provide information on the current and forecasted costs of providing capacity. In turn, the capacity management process also will provide information on charging capacity-related needs and other data for calculating budgeting and charging.

It is important for the cloud consumer to simulate workloads in a cloud environment before the actual movement of the application to the cloud. In the cloud, resources are shared across customers, and in some cloud environments, the architecture of the underlying components is different than that found in traditional IT environments, so it is important that the cloud consumer tests and simulates the application before actual movement to a cloud.

The other aspect during capacity planning has to do with the type of capacity to buy. The following are the options available to the cloud consumer.

- **Lease for a particular period:** This option gives guaranteed capacity to the consumer for a period of time. The costs are less than the option of renting capacity on demand since the consumer is taking a pool of capacity for a longer duration of time.

- **Capacity on demand**: This option provides capacity on a per-hour basis; however, there is no guarantee of availability of new capacity in this model at a particular data center or location since this is market driven.

- **Spot market:** This option allows cloud users to buy capacity provided in the spot market. The prices here are much lower than capacity-on-demand. This option can be used in cases where the application leverages high amounts of compute for processing and can store the results for later processing. In this model the capacity can be taken away from under you if someone outbids you, so it is only fit for scenarios that can process and store results frequently and restart from where they left off, such as drug discovery analysis engines, offline processing engines, etc.

Thus the cloud consumer should take a holistic approach toward capacity requirements in the cloud and not go by the assumption that unlimited capacity will be available as and when required.

A layered strategy with a combination of long term lease, capacity on demand, and spot market buying will give the maximum ROI and ensure that critical applications have enough capacity at the required time.

A hybrid cloud strategy can also be leveraged to provide for further de-risking wherein capacity or availability issues at one cloud provider do not impact the critical applications.

Establishing Architecture

Capacity architecture has major implications on fulfillment of capacity management targets. Here, existing architecture is taken into consideration for a changed service and any modifications or new proposals required are established. This activity is done in conjunction with service level management, security requirements, and availability requirements.

Besides capacity architecture, applications should be developed to consume the lowest possible unit of capacity, unlike conventional applications built with dedicated infrastructure leading to poor resource utilization.

Application scalability is also an important factor when cloud infrastructure is in action. Scalability of an application also allows applications to be scaled up to accommodate the growth. Applications must be intelligently able to speak to underlying infrastructure when the need of more resources like database arises. Application architecture must be supported by both the types of scaling methods, vertical and horizontal. Scaling techniques will be discussed in later sections.

Capacity architecture can be set up to accommodate specific business needs. Let's look at a basic layered capacity architecture view by discussing Figure 8-4.

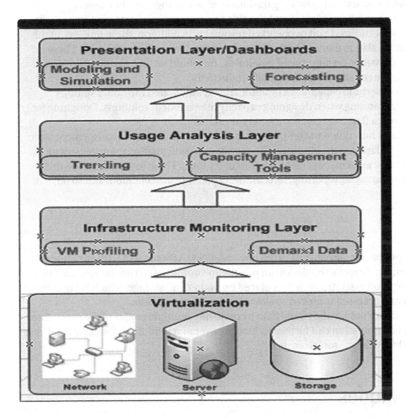

Figure 8-4. *Establish architecture*

Virtualization Tier

At the bottom lies the virtual infrastructure supporting business applications and data. This tier is comprised of the virtual infrastructure, which supports the cloud service.

Infrastructure Monitoring Tier

The infrastructure monitoring tier is the layer that provides monitoring through automated tools for the virtualization tier. This tier gathers the events and performance data for the virtualization tier.

Usage Analysis Tier

The usage analysis tier takes the monitoring data as an input and provides analysis on that data. This layer runs statistical analysis to convert the monitoring data into capacity heat maps, capacity forecasts, and other such analytical reports. Thus, this tier provides the analysis data needed for the cloud provider to make decisions on capacity.

Presentation/Dashboard Tier

The presentation/dashboard tier provides the views for the analytical data generated in the usage analysis tier. This layer allows the capacity managers to use forecasting techniques for generating predictive analysis. This layer also enables capacity managers to do modeling and simulation for understanding the impact of any changes on the capacity.

Presently there are many toolsets that sit at different layers and are able to aggregate, correlate, and present the capacity data to help identify most of the underutilized and overworked resources. In addition, these toolsets, at the forecasting and usage analysis layer, are even able to determine the factors that are driving the workloads. These self-learning toolsets automatically make decisions on automated baselining, threshold setting, alarm settings, etc., and allow users to make the best use of resources and increase IT staff productivity.

Capacity architecture should utilize foreseeable capabilities of self-learning, automated threshold settings, top-down visibility, and proactive capacity planning when designing capacity management solutions. Designing for capacity also specifies the integration and data flow between the toolsets at each tier.

Capacity architecture must clearly specify how different components interact with the capacity management layer. There can be various data collection sources like event monitoring tools, service and configuration management tools, migration tools, application performance tools, asset management, and discovery tools. These toolsets must be able to integrate with capacity management tools for analysis, reporting, forecasting, capacity plan generation, and so on.

Storage Tiering

A tiered storage system offers different types of storage capacity, from low-speed SATA (Serial ATA) drives to high-end solid state drives. The software can automatically move the data from one tier to another based on the rules defined.

Typically data for real time usage that is accessed frequently is placed on higher end storage, which is faster but more costly, and the data that is infrequently accessed is moved to slower and inexpensive disks.

Along with this, de-duplication of data can reduce the actual data by removing multiple copies of the same data and reclaiming the storage capacity. Data compression can further reduce the overall requirement for capacity. These technologies, when used effectively, can bring down storage costs.

Applying Capacity Techniques

Techniques such as component failure impact analysis, application dependency mapping, and management of risk are used to optimize capacity design. A cloud service provider needs a good understanding of his own capacity infrastructure and an ability to predict both capacity and huge fluctuations in demand load. Initially, predictions may be based on rough "rules of thumb" estimates and linear trends, but ultimately they need to be based on scientific methods and application of predictive modeling technologies powered by proven queuing theory algorithms.

There must be simulation of consolidation or virtualization activities brought about by identifying best candidates and targets and optimal placements (for example, according to compatible workloads) with respect to technical, geographical, business, and compliance criteria. Simulations must be able to depict how a service scales from a test environment to a production-level environment by using load testing results. Simulation of infrastructure changes (for example, horizontal or vertical scaling or failover) and business change scenarios must be conducted (for example, business trends and marketing plans).

Detailed techniques and methods on capacity management will be described in later chapters.

Establishing Components and Checking for Cost Optimization

On the basis of prior design activities performed, considerations like use of clusters, etc. are established. Component-level specifications in terms of virtual machine specifications and configuration are performed in line with service performance targets. The capacity database should be integrated with the central IT infrastructure database (called the configuration management database, or CMDB) to establish infrastructural relationships of components with services in action.

A final check in conjunction with financial planning is done to look for available cost-reduction measures without compromising the performance targets. If any measures for cost optimization are identified, they are incorporated. Taking a "virtualize unless otherwise" approach, new and updated apps should be assessed for hosting on the virtualized tier. Updates can include needs for new levels of performance and capacity. Legacy applications on end-of-life hardware should also be evaluated for migration to the virtual tier. A service provider must compare different hardware options with respect to both standard and custom benchmarks and to other criteria such as overall cost or compliance with, for instance, Go Green guidelines. Components for providing capacity can be established as per application needs: criticality, growth, and capacity. Capacity-related needs can be formulated in terms of computing needs. Criticality can be expressed, and levels of fault tolerance and growth can be expressed as future needs. On the basis of application capacity, growth and criticality storage, network and server requirements are formulated. These are coupled with facility requirements.

All these components are summarized in financial terms, and the service provider may provide different service models as per associated costs, which might be gold, silver, and bronze. A gold cost model may include higher Capex but may ensure high performance and reliability. Workloads of mission-critical applications or high capacity seeking applications may be placed in the gold cost model. Similarly workloads like production servers may be placed in silver cost model, and testing, development, cheap and fast deployments may suit the bronze cost model. It is up to the business needs of IT in alignment with financial planning to choose the level of infrastructure capacity that is sought to grow the business. A gold, silver, or bronze service tier represents a baseline—what is good enough to provision a given workload in line with its performance and criticality requirements.

In order to assess the impact of new workloads on capacity, careful assessment of requirements is needed. Infrastructure assessments can be put into practice for getting an infrastructural view on industry wide capability levels.

Since the cloud offers various options for buying capacity, the cost optimization should consider aspects such as

- How much capacity to buy upfront for a longer period since this provides discounted pricing.

- How much capacity on-demand is to be used.

- How to leverage spot instances to lower costs.

- The options for SaaS and overall benefits, and at what point in time the SaaS option will become cheaper or costlier to run as compared to running in a private cloud or IaaS.

As a result, the consumer now has a more complex task at hand due to the different cloud models, vendors, and various pricing options available.

■ ■ ■

CHAPTER 9

Capacity Plan

Once capacity requirements are gathered and finalized, the design for capacity is developed, which primarily includes capacity architecture. This chapter describes how the capacity plan is formed on the basis of capacity design. The capacity plan forms the reference document that is circulated among all stakeholders involved in implementing capacity management procedures. Capacity requirements at all levels (business, service, and component) are documented in the capacity plan.

Steps that must be considered for effective capacity planning in a virtualized/cloud environment are discussed in this chapter. After that, how a capacity plan should be formed and what ingredients are required to create a capacity plan are described.

When rolling out new services in the cloud, the capacity plan is one of the prime artifacts that ensure that benefits of the cloud computing model are reaped effectively. Once a capacity plan is produced, capacity management procedures are implemented in accordance with the plan. A capacity plan is the outcome of procedures discussed in earlier chapters, such as gathering capacity requirements and creating the capacity design. This plan is implemented to keep services live in the most optimum and cost-justifiable way. If a service is already live, the capacity plan constitutes performance and optimization-related metrics and information that keep capacity requirements optimized and tuned.

Producing the Capacity Plan

Figure 9-1 describes the capacity plan inputs and how the capacity plan provides an output for ongoing capacity management. This chapter will list various activities that are needed for producing the capacity plan. The readers can find a sample capacity plan in the Appendix of this book.

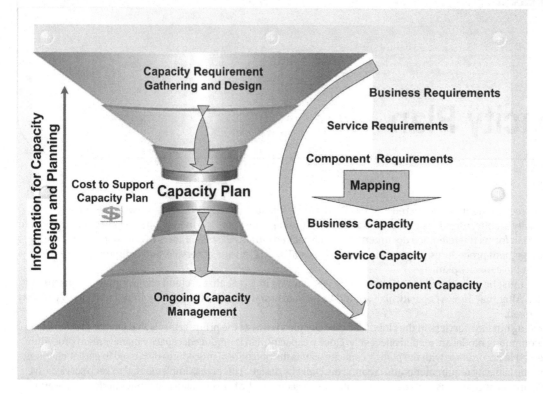

Figure 9-1. *Capacity plan*

Capacity management starts with translating business activities into service requirements for the organization, and then works through the component requirements needed to deliver the specified levels of service.

For effective capacity planning, business needs are first translated into application needs and then these application-related performance and capacity requirements are formulated into infrastructure capacity requirements. These capacity requirements are implemented through capacity design and methods. Different service tiers or packages can be defined by the service provider to provide desired service and performance levels. For example, Gold, Bronze, and Silver service tiers will provide redundant and highly optimized capacity levels to support specific business requirements. These decisions are made using the service levels and financial details that are required to support the required service tier by ensuring that the right capacity is provided at the right time in the most cost-effective way.

Once capacity requirements, design, and architecture are in place, the capacity plan must be produced by infrastructure managers using clear, succinct, relevant information to allow them to allocate resources and capital where it will deliver the most business benefit.

Let's first elaborate on the steps that must be considered for effective capacity planning in cloud environment.

Identifying the Profiles of Virtual Machines

There are various ways of grouping or standardizing the profiles, which are provided as templates for provisioning of virtual machines. The profiles will be comprised of the compute resources made available initially to the virtual machine along with other things like the operating system version, applications, or packages pre-installed on the template. It is important to include the capacity planning aspects in the template.

As an example, there are minimum requirements for a specific type of OS and database, so based on the application usage, the capacity of that template can be decided upon. Different instances of the same template may increase the capacity to accommodate for usage scenarios that scale out.

At the end of this exercise we will have a list of profiles with all of the required details available.

Identifying Host Server Profiles

The host servers on which the virtual machines are placed can be grouped based on important attributes like the compute capacity available and the intended usage. As an example, hosts can be differentiated based on the type of service that they offer, such as database server, web server, or middleware server.

The servers may also be configured to be in a pool that serves a specific purpose and has security and firewalls configured accordingly. As an example, you may create a pool of web servers and another pool of database servers and have these two pools separated by a firewall. The network configuration of the web servers allows them access from outside the internal network, while the network configuration of the database servers makes them accessible only internally.

Identifying Storage

Storage profiling includes the type of storage disks based on performance and the storage system based on the connectivity to the host pool, as described above. Thus, storage is connected to a group of hosts based on the requirements of the workload being placed on those hosts. As an example, the storage on a database workload may be of higher performance and may leverage faster disks to give better performance, while for web servers it may not be of a similar performance level. The storage profile will include the RAID Configuration, LUN Configuration, network configuration, and types of storage like SATA, SAS, and fiber channel.

Developing Thresholds and Alerting

Threshold and alerting definitions are created for various components and services including networks, storage, CPU, and memory. This involves defining the various performance metrics and the thresholds for these metrics. The thresholds may be multiple and may trigger different states, such as *warning* or *critical*.

Let's say the CPU of a host is being used up to 90 percent over the last one hour. This may trigger a warning alert so that appropriate action can be taken by the administrators to avoid performance degradation.

Resource Replenishment

In the highly dynamic environments of cloud computing, resource replenishment is an ongoing activity and a huge challenge. Since the usage pattern and the business activities aggregate of a lot of customers, it becomes a challenge for the cloud provider to define how resource replenishment will occur. Not having enough resources to meet the customers demand will result in loss of revenue and profitability plus loss of customers as they may go elsewhere to procure capacity. Thus, cloud providers will typically have extra capacity to provide elasticity features and on-demand compute to its customers.

The cloud provider needs to have highly automated systems and back-end integration with the providers to provision capacity automatically and to procure capacity through ordering based on statistical and automated analysis of the utilization data.

Demand Management and Forecasting

As described above, it is essential for cloud providers to have highly automated and rich systems to do demand management and forecasting. Complex algorithms and systems are developed to provide demand management and forecasting of demand. The following analysis is required for a cloud provider to anticipate and forecast demand:

- Demand during time of day
- Demand during day of the week
- Demand during day of the month
- Seasonal variation
- Special days (Christmas or Cyber Monday)
- Demand from different time zones
- Demand for different locations/data centers
- Resource pools

The compute and storage resources are grouped under resource pools so that the allocation of virtual machines that require the resources characterized by these resource pools are can happen to these resource pools. These are essentially groupings of cloud resources based on certain attributes like the type of workloads. As an example, a resource pool may be created for development environments that have hosts, storage, etc. allocated, and all development machines will be allocated resources from this pool.

Creating a Capacity Plan

Now let's discuss an approach to create a capacity plan. These procedures or activities may vary depending upon an enterprise's nomenclature and policies but these activities can be referred to whenever a capacity plan is prepared. The procedures for producing a capacity plan are as follows:

- Document capacity requirements.
- Document design and methods used.
- Produce the overall plan.

Document Capacity Requirements

Cloud service providers must define roles and responsibilities to facilitate information gathering for capacity calculations, and this information is documented in a standard template called the *capacity plan*. This plan must be managed and maintained through regular updates, information validations, document control checks, and version management.

Capacity requirements are translated from business to service to component levels, and associated SLAs like performance targets of business, service, and component parameters are documented in the capacity plan. Business SLAs like service availability, performance, and monitoring are clearly mentioned in the capacity plan.

Service SLAs must be translated from business to service. For example, providing a business SLA of service availability should be backed by service support SLAs like response time and resolution times. Component SLAs can include OLAs with third parties. Multi-vendor SLAs and OLAs were covered in earlier chapters.

Capacity planners need to clearly establish dependency mappings between the business requirements like service availability or performance and service support requirements. Similarly, mapping between service requirements and resource consumption must be calculated and documented. User profiles and task matrices must be calculated and documented. Forecasting on the basis of service consumption trends is done and documented in a capacity plan to handle future demand spikes. Cloud service providers can use scaling algorithms to understand business requirements in order to provide optimum capacity for up/down scaling options, which are cost justifiable and support desired service levels. Capacity modeling can be used to forecast the behavior of infrastructure using demand, financial, virtual, operational, software, and vendor data. The right capacity management strategy for the cloud computing business is dependent on target customer profiles as they bear the cost of availed capacity.

Things to look at when gathering capacity requirements:

- Who is the customer?

- What value is being delivered?

- What feature set the customer is seeking with implications on capacity management, like scalability, cloud bursting, application mobility, high availability, fault tolerance, production workloads, and agreed SLAs?

Understanding internal capacity competencies and those of your target clients will help you more accurately predict customer's capacity requirements. Doing ideal capacity sizing is still a challenge, but a cloud service provider must adopt the use of best practices, models, and software tools. The probabilities of success for capacity management in cloud service will be maximized. Having tools that provide the visibility and control into the cloud and allow cloud providers to measure and report on actual capacity usage per customer will set the class of cloud service apart and ensure the maximized profitability.

There are capacity planning tools to map application dependency on infrastructure, to describe the criticality of each application and SLA thresholds and organize applications as per the service tiers. The cloud provider has to be very logical when mapping the service tiers within the infrastructure at hand. Emerging concepts like *self-learning, yield management, and capacity optimization* help cloud providers to establish optimized capacity requirements. If different service tiers rely on the same infrastructure, the service provider may consider restructuring to align capacity with criticality after business needs are identified and documented. These capacity management requirements are backed by capacity management techniques and tools. See later sections for implementation techniques.

At the component level, the capacity plan must include information on CPU, memory, input or output, network, storage, and usage needs. The service provider must ensure that SLA-, application-, infrastructure-, and vendor-related information is gathered and documented and that it contributes to the overall capacity plan. Besides this workload analysis, utilization analysis, response time analysis, etc. must be taken into account.

It is important to ensure that capacity planning is done to regulate component level demand by using balancing factors of peak-to-average loads to identify those CIs (configuration items) that might be candidates for balancing. CIs with extremely high usage are good candidates for demand balancing. Comparing the average load of a CI with its peak hour load identifies such candidates and creates a metric for this balance of peak-to-average load and ensures that it will be tracked as a part of capacity planning.

Document Design and Methods Used

Methods and techniques used to arrive at the design to support capacity requirements must be mentioned in the capacity plan. These capacity designs must be based on basic principles of data center architecture and cost justifications. This includes techniques and methodologies that support performance, scalability, and availability in cloud environments like load balancing, clustering, and resource allocation. Virtual machine population profiles must be designed to optimally support running business applications.

The reporting aspects should cover the over-sized and under-sized virtual machines. Over-sized virtual machines are using less capacity compared to what has been allocated to the virtual machine. Under-sized machines are starved of compute capacity and are facing capacity constraints that may hamper the application performance of applications running on those virtual machines. Reporting of these conditions will result in providing capacity where it is most needed. Techniques for capacity design implementation will be discussed in detail in ongoing capacity management sections.

The finally concluded design, including architecture, design measures, and capacity details, also must be mentioned. Business-to-service-to-component-level mapping should be done and with required performance SLAs at all levels. As discussed in an earlier section, multi-vendor environment SLAs, OLAs, and UCs must be well defined, and the capacity management design and methods should be able to justify the same.

The justification for how the proposed design is to be deployed supports the business and user requirements in terms of SLA, with detailed mapping and supporting calculations documented in the capacity plan. Third-party OLAs and UCs must be considered when designing capacity management architecture so that the capacity calculations for supporting SLAs are accurate.

Producing the Overall Plan

After all the ingredients of the capacity plan are ready and decided upon, information gathering activities are carried out to collate the information from various shareholders. Before the data collection phase of the capacity management plan, it must have an organized template or other format to collect data (including business/service/component SLAs, application, infrastructure, vendor-related information, service tiers, and so on). These must be clearly mentioned in the capacity plan.

Important sections of a capacity plan include the following:

- **SLAs:** This section includes agreed service levels that the cloud provider commits to the customer.

- **Applications:** This must include the data regarding each of the organization's applications. It must also be ensured that all applications have been accounted for and that the information regarding each application is correct.

- **Current Infrastructure:** This section includes data regarding the data center's virtual and physical assets. It must also ensure that all devices have been accounted for and that the information regarding each device is correct.

- **User Task Scenarios:** Usage scenarios (also called use cases) define the sequences of tasks users perform and their interactions with solution functions to help them to perform these tasks. This section of the capacity plan should define the scenarios that are worked upon by the user in each respective functional area. Identifying and describing usage scenarios provides details that enable the estimation of capacity loads and other factors.

- **Task Load Matrix:** The task–load matrix describes the different kinds of load that each usage scenario puts on the system.

- **Monitoring and Metrics:** The monitoring and metrics section describes the monitoring methods, techniques, and tools that will be used to evaluate solution and component performance and provides metrics for planning intervention. This information should be provided for each major component at the solution level.

- **Forecasts:** The business plans should provide capacity management with details of the new services planned and the growth or contraction in the use of existing services. This subsection should report on new services and the demise of legacy systems.

- **Service Tiers:** Responsible for creating service packages or service levels that are based on a pre-established set of application-critical criteria, such as a Gold service tier for the most critical applications.

- **Supplier Information:** Responsible for collecting contact information from vendors and internal contacts so that they are readily available during a capacity crisis.

Once the capacity plan is drafted, it is circulated among all stakeholders in a non-ambiguous and accessible format presenting component, service, and business views for implementation in ongoing capacity management. Once the capacity plan is formulated, capacity management toolsets are deployed and all capacity-related parameters like thresholds, alerts, notifications, and service levels are configured.

At this stage, the capacity management process takes a new turn and focus moves from capacity planning of a new service to ongoing capacity management. In Chapter 10, you will see how ongoing capacity management works and you'll learn the techniques and methods to carry out the same.

See the Appendix for a capacity plan template.

CHAPTER 10

■■■

Ongoing Capacity Management for Existing or Live Services

Once capacity requirements are gathered and finalized, the capacity management process ensures that the capacity plan is implemented as drafted in the plan document. This phase of capacity management is focused on implementation of capacity architecture and design. This chapter emphasizes implementing techniques like scaling, clustering, ballooning, and load balancing, which play vital roles in ensuring that capacity levels support specified service levels. All these techniques are specific to virtual environments and provide flexibility in managing capacity. This phase of capacity management is called *iterative capacity management*. Figure 10-1 includes steps like implementing capacity techniques, monitoring capacity/performance metrics, analyzing capacity data, and capacity tuning. This chapter exclusively covers implementation of capacity techniques in cloud based/virtualized environments.

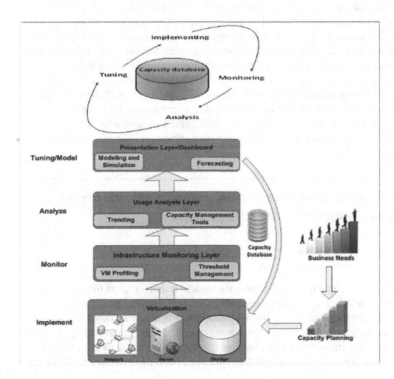

Figure 10-1. *Iterative capacity management*

Once all the options for calculating requirements in support of a new service are in place and documented in the capacity plan, capacity management takes a new turn in implementing the capacity design techniques, managing ongoing performance optimization, and monitoring.

After capacity planning is done and services are rolled out, capacity implementation procedures are invoked. The capacity plan serves as a reference document for implementation of iterative capacity management procedures and techniques.

An important consideration for ongoing capacity management is the ever-changing business requirements, which generate associated capacity requirements in capacity planning for ongoing or live services. Hence there exists the need for end-to-end monitoring and analysis of a virtualized environment. Monitoring and analysis of infrastructure usage by customers are two prime areas of iterative capacity management, followed by tuning and (if required) implementation of changes to fine tune the monitoring.

Tooling and monitoring requirements will need to be re-evaluated prior to moving to a cloud implementation, as the traditional capacity focus at the component level will become less important with an aggregated service view being the key to understanding service performance and usage. When selecting a tool, it should be ensured that it will monitor systems and services across the enterprise and have the flexibility to import a wide variety of data sources. These information sources can then be used to provide a unified reporting portal to assist in capacity monitoring and planning for the cloud, and service. In a cloud implementation, rather than the components being the first bottleneck, it is likely the network will be the focal point for initial performance monitoring and planning, more specifically the network links between the customer and the cloud provider (CP).

Depending upon the cloud environment and cost considerations, cloud providers have to decide upon the best of breed toolsets to use to perform ongoing capacity management. This may include configuring and integrating multiple toolsets to perform specialized performance management functions like monitoring, analysis, and forecasting. Cloud providers can either go with implementing multiple toolsets and synchronizing them to perform capacity monitoring, analysis, and tuning, or go with a unified capacity management solution. The objective is to monitor the environment, generate monitoring data, analyze it, and tune the capacity optimization actions.

These activities provide the basic historical information and triggers necessary for all of the other activities and processes within capacity management. Monitors should be established on all components for each of the services. The data should be analyzed using, wherever possible, expert systems to compare usage levels against thresholds. The results of the analysis should be included in reports, and recommendations made as appropriate. Some form of control mechanism may then be put in place to act on the recommendations. This may take the form of balancing services, balancing workloads, changing concurrency levels, and adding or removing resources. All of the information accumulated during these activities should be stored in the Capacity Management Information System (CMIS) and the cycle then begins again, monitoring any changes made to ensure they have had a beneficial effect and collecting more data for future actions.

Capacity managers must make time to learn new ways of doing their job and investigating new technologies so they can make prudent decisions when it is time to implement a new system or perform an upgrade. Each new technology needs to be assessed for its value to the business.

 The implementation side of capacity management in a cloud environment must primarily consider infrastructure scaling procedures and algorithms in the virtualization layer.

An important consideration here is VM sprawl. Since the cloud makes it easy and quick for users to spin new capacity on demand, there may be times when virtual machines are ordered but not relinquished post usage. This leads to wasted resources as the machines are not used. There should be monitoring of virtual machines for their usage. Based on the usage trends, the ones that are not used for long durations need to be marked as Sprawl and appropriate actions need to be taken. This is important to ensure that optimum and required capacity is consumed by various departments and users and that unused capacity is reclaimed. VM sprawl can add unnecessary costs for an enterprise consuming cloud services.

Implementation

It was the process of implementing the identified changes or new capacity that was forecasted during the monitoring, analysis, and tuning activities. The objective of the implementation activity is to introduce to the live services any changes that have been identified by the monitoring, analysis, and tuning activities. The implementation of any changes arising from these activities must undergo a strict, formal change management process. The impact of system tuning changes can have major implications on the customers of the service. The impact and risk associated with these types of changes are likely to be greater than that of different types of changes. Implementing the capacity plan may include the following activities:

- **Identify implementation requirements:** Any capacity addition/removal/reconfiguration is evaluated in terms of its impact on current service operations. Any requirements in terms of technical configuration, procurement of hardware and software, cost of implementation, licensing requirements, and skills required for implementation are identified to achieve the desired objective of the proposed implementation project.

- **Identify monitoring requirements:** Evaluate the impact of the proposed implementation (addition/removal/reconfiguration) in terms of the ability to monitor the performance of capacity parameters. Requirements are identified in terms of tools (mechanisms) required to monitor the performance and integration of the proposed implementation with the current monitoring environment.

- **Identify reporting requirements:** Reporting requirements as defined in the capacity management process are identified. Integrations required with ITSM systems, monitoring systems, and so on are documented to generate the capacity reports.

- **Translate requirements to specifications:** Identified requirements are evaluated, and a decision based on a holistic view of all requirements is made to produce specifications.

- **Develop a project plan:** This phase involves development of a project plan for implementation of the activities identified.

Scaling

Scaling is the ability to increase or decrease compute capacity either by launching additional servers or changing server sizes. The following infrastructure scaling procedures, techniques, and algorithms used in virtualization layer techniques are considered in order to implement capacity management. These techniques are based on the high levels of automation that virtualization brings to cloud environments.

Horizontal scaling

Horizontal scaling is the ability to automatically scale (grow or shrink) the number of server resources that are provisioned in a particular deployment. For example, as a site grows and the number of user requests increases, you can scale up horizontally by launching and provisioning additional server resources to serve your application (Figure 10-2). Conversely, when those resources are no longer needed, you can scale down and automatically terminate underutilized server resources.

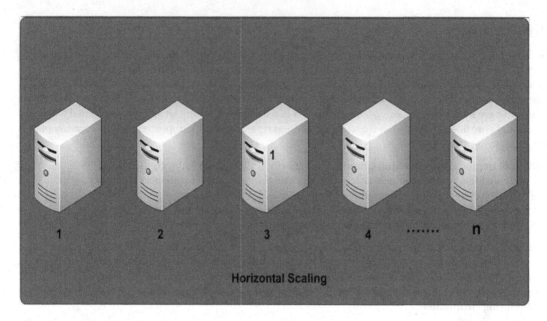

Figure 10-2. *Horizontal scaling*

Vertical scaling

Vertical scaling is the ability to scale the size of a server (Figure 10-3). This is another way to dramatically change compute capacity. Depending on the customer site's architecture, cost, and bandwidth requirements, it might be more beneficial for you to scale vertically instead of horizontally. For example, instead of managing six smaller servers, you might want to simplify your deployment and replace them with two larger servers that provide an equivalent amount of performance at a more cost-effective rate. Vertical scaling is also common for growing the size of your database over time. Unlike horizontal scaling, some cloud providers or solutions may not provide for automatic vertical scaling.

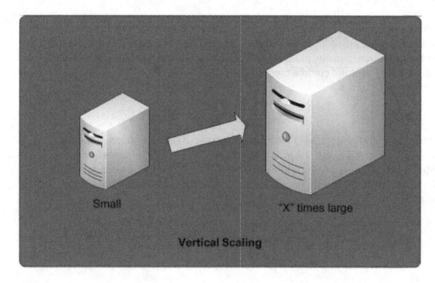

Figure 10-3. *Vertical scaling*

Auto scaling

Auto scaling allows scaling capacity to go up or down automatically as per the conditions you define. With auto scaling, you can ensure that the number of instances running increases seamlessly during demand spikes to maintain performance and decreases automatically during demand lulls to minimize costs. Examples of metrics on which you can set conditions include average CPU utilization, network activity, or disk utilization.

To use auto scaling, the applications must be architected in a loosely coupled manner and must support horizontal scaling. Auto scaling is suited for applications that experience hourly, daily, or weekly variability in usage. Auto scaling can be achieved by defining the alert conditions under which additional servers will be launched or terminated. There are two different ways of configuring auto scaling:

- **Alert-based:** Defines alerts that are monitored on the server (for example, if a CPU is idle at less than 30% for 10 minutes). When an alert condition's threshold has been met or exceeded, an alert is triggered and the auto scaling uses this alert to scale up or down the instances.

- **Queue-based:** These are for grid systems wherein the queue master can spin new machines on the grid based on the number of items pending in the queue. The alert is set to the number of active items in the queue; if it exceeds a certain value, the number of machines in the grid can be increased to accommodate more requests.

Clustering

A server cluster (Figure 10-4) aggregates the capacity of two or more servers and creates a virtual resource. A server cluster improves performance by aggregating the capacity of two or more physical machines. An active passive server clustering configuration provides for high availability wherein if an active node fails, the passive node takes over the workload of the active node that went down. An active configuration, on the other hand, provides ways and means to scale out the capacity using the cluster as the multiple servers work together to share the workload.

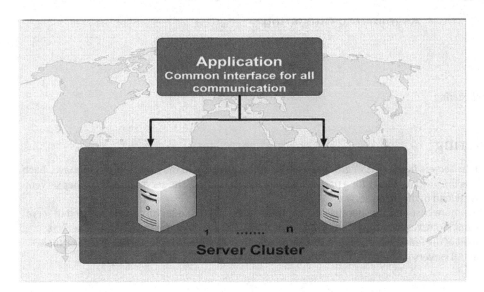

Figure 10-4. *Clustering*

Asymmetric clustering

The active passive cluster as described above is also known as an asymmetric cluster wherein a standby server exists only to take over for another server in the event of failure. This type of cluster is usually used to provide high availability and scalability for read or write stores such as databases, messaging systems, and file and print services.

The standby server performs no other useful work and is either as capable as or less capable than a primary server. A less capable, less expensive standby server is often used in this scenario when the primary servers are themselves in high availability mode and have redundant systems. This type of configuration is also called a failover configuration.

Figure 10-5 shows an asymmetric configuration. Under normal conditions, the primary server handles all requests. In the event of a failure, the standby server takes over and the applications continue to function.

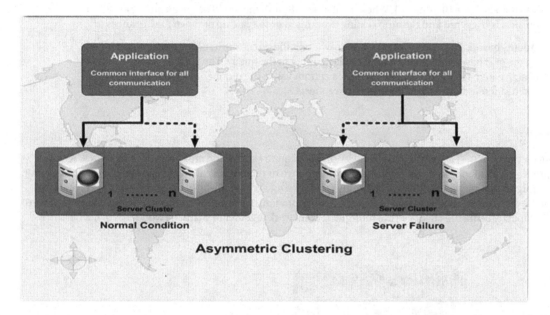

Figure 10-5. *Asymetric clustering*

Symmetric clustering

In symmetric clusters, all the servers in the cluster group are active and participate in the processing of requests. Each server may be designated as the primary server for a particular set of applications. If the server fails, the other servers in the group take up the workload of the failed server.

Symmetric clusters are more cost-effective because the compute resources of the servers are being used to serve active applications and users. However, care must be taken to ensure that in case of failure the remaining servers are able to take the workload of the failed server. Figure 10-6 illustrates how a symmetric cluster presents a virtual resource to an application. All servers participate in handling transactions.

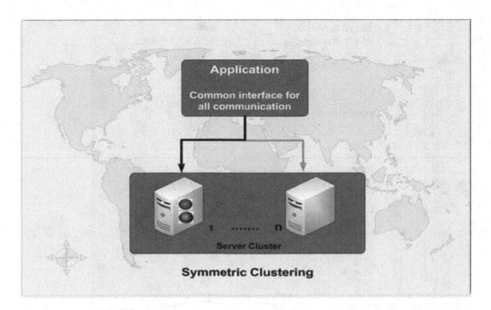

Figure 10-6. *Symetric clustering*

One common type of symmetric cluster is a load-balanced cluster. A load-balanced cluster enhances the performance, availability, and scalability of services such as web servers, media servers, and read-only databases by distributing requests across all the servers that are part of the symmetric cluster.

Load Balancing

Load balancers, as the name suggests, provides load balancing across multiple servers. A load balancer balances the load coming from the users or applications to the back-end servers (Figure 10-7). The load balancer hides the back-end servers and exposes a single URL/IP address for applications or users and manages the connections to multiple back-end servers.

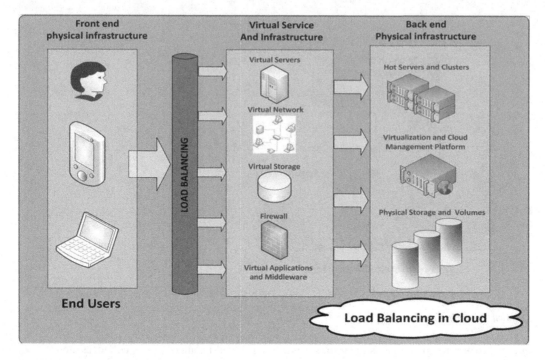

Figure 10-7. *Load balancing*

A load balancer is a key piece in the scalability scenario as it provides front-end applications with the capability to scale out to multiple servers without impacting the users. The users /applications connect to the load balancer, which decides based on various options which server gets the traffic and transactions.

A load balancer also enables scalability because now back-end servers can be provisioned or de-provisioned without requiring changes to the network or downtime of the application. The load balancer sends requests only to the healthy servers in the network and enables optimum utilization of the back-end servers while at the same time providing high availability. It automatically handles the increases and decreases in capacity and adapts its distribution decisions based on the capacity available at the time a request is made.

One of the most common applications of load balancing is to provide a single Internet service from multiple servers, which is sometimes known as a server farm. An alternate method of load balancing that does not necessarily require a dedicated software or hardware node is called a round-robin DNS. In this technique, multiple IP addresses are associated with a single domain name (for example, `www.example.org`) and clients themselves are expected to choose the server they want to connect to. Unlike the use of a dedicated load balancer, this technique exposes to clients the existence of multiple back-end servers. This technique has other advantages and disadvantages, depending on the degree of control over the DNS server and the granularity of load balancing desired.

Typically, a load balancing configuration decides how to choose and where to send the request. The following are some of the common load balancer configurations:

- **Round Robin:** This is the simplest method where each server takes a turn. The load balancer starts from the first server, and each subsequent request is sent to the next server in the round robin.

- **Weighted:** Typically, servers are allocated a percentage capability as one server could be twice as powerful as another. Weighted methods are useful if the load balancer does not know the real and actual performance of the server.

- **Least Connections:** The load balancer will keep track of the number of connections a server has and send the next request to the server that has the least connections.

- **Fastest Response:** This type of method is available in high-end load balancing where the load balancer takes into consideration the time each server is taking to respond and then decides to send the request to the server providing the fastest response time.

The two major categories of load balancing implementations are the following:

- **Software-based Load Balancing:** This consists of special software that is installed on the servers in a load-balanced cluster. The software is responsible for the load balancing functionality and redirects the requests received from clients to the backend servers based on the configuration. For example, Microsoft's Network Load Balancing is load balancing software for web farms, and Microsoft's Component Load Balancing is load balancing software for application farms.

- **Hardware-based Load Balancing:** This consists of specialized hardware with software to give it load balancing functionality. Typically these devices are high end and provide for advanced configurations and support heavy throughput.

Memory Ballooning

Memory ballooning is a technique by which the hypervisor can reduce the memory pressure on the host machines. It is a reclamation technique that takes the inactive or unused host physical memory away from the idle virtual machines and gives it to other virtual machines that will actively use it. Since the virtual machine operating system is isolated from the host and the other virtual machines running on the same host, it is unaware of the memory available on the host and the memory usage of the other virtual machines on the same host. When the free host memory becomes low, none of the virtual machines will free guest physical memory because the guest operating system has no way of detecting the load on the host. This is where memory ballooning comes into play and makes the guest OS aware of the low memory on the host. This is achieved by a driver being placed in the guest OS, which connects the guest OS to the hypervisor and thus enables this communication. The memory balloon driver inflates the balloon by requesting the guest OS to release physical memory so that the same can be allocated to the balloon and thus to the other virtual machines that need the memory at that point in time (Figure 10-8).

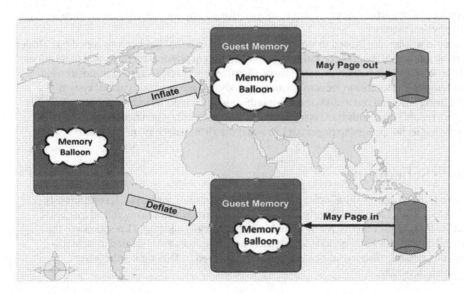

Figure 10-8. *Ballooning*

The guest operating system interface decides the pages to be marked for ballooning to take over and thus has complete control over the memory it manages for its own use. The hypervisor reclaims host physical memory in a manner that ensures that no guest process can access these memory pages after they are marked for ballooning. The hypervisor inflates the memory balloon when it has less memory. By inflating the balloon, the virtual machine's consumption of the host physical memory goes down since it releases memory to the balloon. However, this results in usage of more physical memory on the guest machine. Thus ballooning transfers the memory pressure to the guest machine. The guest operating system is required to have a memory ballooning driver for the ballooning to work. The guest operating system needs to have virtual swap space configured for guest paging.

VMware Ballooning

An ESX server (hypervisor) controls a balloon module running within the guest, directing it to allocate guest pages and pin them in "physical" memory. The machine pages backing this memory can then be reclaimed by the ESX server. Inflating the balloon increases memory pressure, forcing the guest OS to invoke its own memory management algorithms. The guest OS may page out to its virtual disk when memory is scarce. Deflating the balloon decreases pressure, freeing guest memory.

VMware's balloon driver, also known as the vmmemctl driver, collaborates with the server to reclaim pages that are considered least valuable by the guest OS. It essentially acts like a native program in the OS that requires more and more memory. The driver uses a proprietary ballooning technique that provides predictable performance that closely matches the behavior of a native system under similar memory constraints. This technique effectively increases or decreases memory pressure on the guest OS, causing the guest to invoke its own native memory management algorithms. When memory is tight, the guest OS decides which particular pages to reclaim and, if necessary, swaps them to its own virtual disk. You need to be sure your guest's OS has sufficient swap space. This swap space must be greater than or equal to the difference between the virtual machine's configured memory size and its reservation.

When your host runs low on memory, ESXi uses the memory balloon driver within the guest OS to force it to use its own paging system and thus free up memory that the host can use. The use of the balloon driver will subsequently lead to increased disk input or output as the guest OS pages out low priority memory to disk.

Swapping

Swapping algorithms allow processes or portions of processes to move between physical memory and a mass storage device. This frees up space in physical memory.

An area of a disk (for example, a swap file) is used to store the state of a process that has been swapped out. Under a virtual memory system, it is the amount of swap space rather than the amount of physical memory that determines the maximum size of a single process and the maximum total size of all active processes. Swapping is mostly used when the ballooning driver is temporarily unable to reclaim memory quickly enough to satisfy current system demand. Since the memory is being swapped out to disk, there is a rather significant performance penalty when this technique is used. Swapping is a reliable mechanism of last resort that a host uses only when necessary to reclaim memory. Standard-demand paging techniques swap pages back in when the virtual machine needs them.

Distributed Resource Scheduling

Distributed Resource Scheduler (DRS) dynamically allocates and balances computing resources. It continuously monitors utilization across a resource pool and intelligently allocates available resources among virtual machines according to operational and business requirements. Along with this, it dynamically allocates IT resources to the highest priority applications and creates rules and policies to prioritize how resources are allocated to virtual machines (Figure 10-9). Thus, the dynamic resource allocation method employed by DRS makes the job of virtualization and cloud administrators easy.

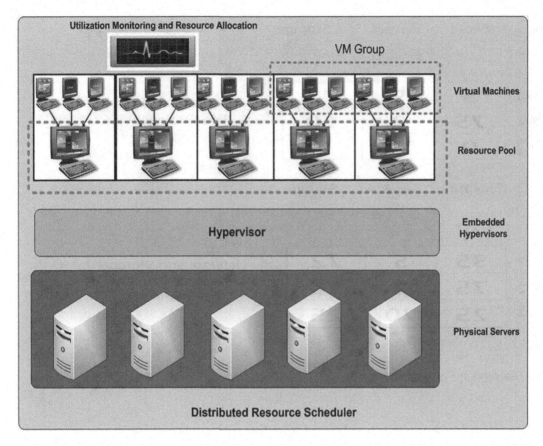

Figure 10-9. *Distributed Resource Scheduler*

Based on the consumption of resources, the DRS moves virtual machines to the correct hosts and thus maximizes the usage of cloud resources. This, coupled with dynamic power management, can bring down power costs. Dynamic power management can shut down servers during off-peak hours after moving the workload to other servers.

Time Zones and Variable Workloads

One of the key areas to be looked at in the cloud computing landscape is how a cloud service provider handles multiple capacity requirements in different time zones at a given time. The cloud service provider needs to be proactive enough to anticipate utilization requirements coming from various geographies. For instance, a financial application running from the Asia Pacific region may seek high resource requirements in terms of higher computing capability during business hours and, at the same time, there might be requirements by a pharmaceutical for high-bandwidth data transfer and storage for weekly backups. In situations like these, cloud service providers must consider all these geo-specific business requirements and design the service model in which there are none or the least possible bottlenecks or resource conflicts. This is depicted in Figure 10-10.

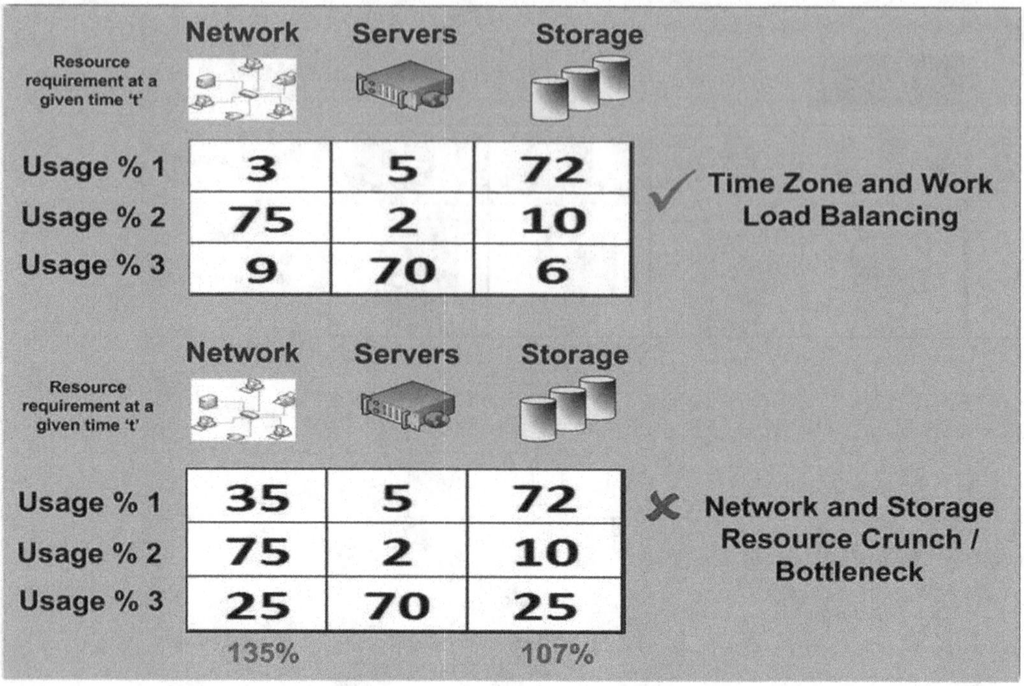

	Network	Servers	Storage	
Resource requirement at a given time 't'				
Usage % 1	3	5	72	✓ Time Zone and Work
Usage % 2	75	2	10	Load Balancing
Usage % 3	9	70	6	

	Network	Servers	Storage	
Resource requirement at a given time 't'				
Usage % 1	35	5	72	✗ Network and Storage
Usage % 2	75	2	10	Resource Crunch /
Usage % 3	25	70	25	Bottleneck
	135%		107%	

Figure 10-10. *Time zones and variable workloads*

CHAPTER 11

Capacity Monitoring

After capacity management techniques are implemented as per the service levels mentioned in the capacity plan, it becomes critical to constantly monitor the cloud environment. This chapter on cloud capacity management talks exclusively about the monitoring of cloud-based environments. Monitoring the cloud environment is the core of performance management. The monitoring data collected forms the basis of further capacity planning, so it is critical for any cloud service provider to monitor the cloud environment. This chapter also describes various monitoring entities and metrics that service providers must consider while doing performance management. Besides supporting capacity, monitoring data also provides meaningful information required by other service management processes like event management, incident management, and problem management.

Monitoring

This chapter will discuss monitoring at the component layer and how it impacts the capacity planning in the cloud environment. This monitoring activity triggers capacity planning activities like input/output tuning, workload balancing, and storage fine-tuning.

In a cloud environment, the monitoring activities are performed using specialized tools in an automated fashion. The monitoring tools monitor the various components that comprise the cloud service for attributes like CPU usage, disk usage, memory usage, and network usage. The monitoring activity is a part of the event management process, and the inputs on what parameters to monitor, what thresholds to set, and how to aggregate and analyze the performance data are provided from the capacity management process during the design phase.

Capacity management involves the utilization of each resource and service being monitored on an ongoing basis to ensure that cloud resources are being used optimally and that all agreed-upon service levels can be achieved. Most monitoring tasks are near-term in nature and rely on tools and monitoring principles for operation. The collected information is recorded or sampled over a pre-determined period. The amount of sampling and resources required to do so are also examined.

The Capacity Management Database (CDB) contains data points to identify historical trends and patterns. Data is gathered not only at the total resource utilization level, but also at a more detailed level for the workload on each particular resource up to the extent it is optimally possible to do so by the tools. This is carried out across the whole infrastructure, including applications, servers, and networks. Similarly, data is collected for each service, such as availability and user screen response time. The data from monitoring is matched against a baseline and normal operating levels; any breaches of thresholds and abnormal behavior against baselines are translated to an alarm and exceptions are generated.

Some of the entities that are of prime importance for capacity monitoring include:

- CPU and memory utilization

- IOPS

- Device utilization

- Queue length

- Storage utilization

- Transaction rate

- Network packet rate

- Application response time

- Bandwidth utilization

There is a difference between the information collected around managing capacity and the data required for performance monitoring. The capacity data is more granular, typically five minutes, and this raw data is fed to capacity planning systems to generated capacity charts, heat charts, and trends of capacity using various statistical methods. It is important to take care of changes happening in the environment and their impact on monitoring, since a change to the base infrastructure may result in invalidation of the past data or the data may need recalibration to provide meaningful analysis. Thus, changes to the infrastructure or monitoring tools or parameters need to be carefully analyzed to see the impact on past baselines.

A major value of capacity monitoring and analysis is that the information collected can be used to predict future activity by predicting future resource usage and by monitoring actual business growth against predicted growth. This provides the intelligence to the business to make decisions for capacity in a timely manner and thus reduce costs.

Utilization Monitoring

As discussed above, monitoring must involve toolsets that are deployed in a cloud environment and it must collect data specific to particular applications and underlying infrastructure including the operating system. The monitoring tools must be able to identify the service and its components so that service-specific components are monitored; these components may include the following:

- CPU

- Memory

- IOPS

- Disk storage

- Transaction rates

- Response times

- Hit rates

- Concurrent user numbers

- Network traffic

CPU Demand

CPU demand takes into account a virtual machine's CPU usage and its CPU ready and CPU wait times to derive the CPU capacity demand for the virtual machine.

Memory Demand

Memory demand considers memory consumed by a virtual machine, which reflects any ballooning, page sharing, and memory swapping for the virtual machine, as well as memory overheads due to virtualization, to derive the memory capacity demand for the virtual machine.

The capacity management tool has various sources of data to capture. Some of the hypervisor managers collect the basic performance data on the CPU, memory, disk, and network consumption by virtual machines. The capacity planning tool can integrate and pick up this data from the hypervisor management system like vCenter. The capacity management tool can also use agentless and agent-based systems to collect data from the virtual machines and networks to store it and perform capacity analysis using statistical algorithms.

The capacity management tool maintains a capacity database where the capacity data is stored. The capacity management tool does aggregation of data into hourly and daily buckets for analysis.

Advanced capacity management tools also provide features to simulate the working of an application on increased or decreased capacity. Such tools also maintain detailed descriptions of capacity details of server models and hypervisor performance from leading vendors to enable them to analyze the data in greater detail.

The capacity management tool also takes into account capacity reserved for failover, virtualization overhead, or any capacity headroom you may need.

Usable capacity = Total capacity − Unusable capacity

The used capacity can be obtained in one of the following two ways:

- Total host resources used

- Total usable host resources

The capacity planning tool provides extensive reporting capabilities including:

- Trend reports

- Forecasting using various algorithms

- Capacity hot spots

- Underutilized capacity reports

- Facility for ad hoc reporting

- Capacity alerts

Total virtual machine capacity

Total virtual machine capacity is the sum of deployed and remaining virtual machine capacity.

Total virtual machine count capacity = Deployed virtual machine capacity + Remaining virtual machine capacity

Deployed virtual machine capacity

Deployed virtual machine capacity is the number of virtual machines already deployed in the datacenter or cluster. Deployed virtual machines include virtual machines regardless of whether they have been powered on or off.

Remaining virtual machine capacity

Remaining virtual machine capacity is a measure of the number of new virtual machines that can be deployed. The remaining virtual machine capacity value is based on the assumptions that the capacity management tool makes about capacity demands of new or future virtual machines you expect to deploy.

For example, a typical deployment of virtual machines would include a mix of small, medium, and large, with varying capacities on the CPUs, memory, and disks.The capacity analysis at the cloud level will use the mix of virtual machines and calculate the seasonal variations, day-wise variations, and time variations on the usage of these virtual machines along with the demand forecast to arrive at the capacity requirements for the cloud.

The capacity analysis on virtual machines is based on the average virtual machine capacity of the types of virtual machines available on the cloud. As an example, if you have 10 virtual machines and 50% are small, 30% are medium, and 20% are large, then the average virtual machine CPU demand = 0.5 x (CPU demand for small virtual machines) + 0.3 x (CPU demand for medium virtual machines) + 0.2 x (CPU demand for large virtual machines). The result of the average virtual machine CPU demand and average virtual machine memory demand represents the average virtual machine profile for this cluster (Figure 11-1). This is used for capacity planning based on the size of virtual machines and arrives at the overall requirement of CPU, memory, and storage for the cloud (see Figure 11-1).

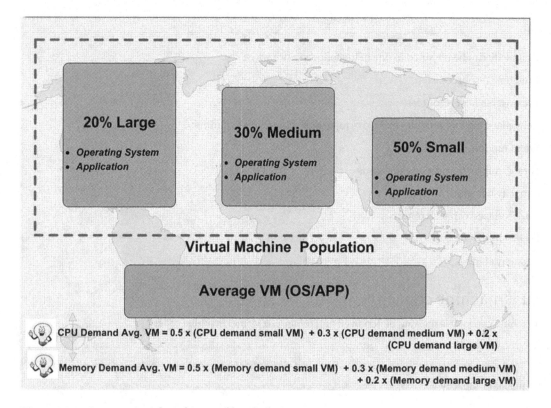

Figure 11-1. *Average virtual machine profile calculation*

The remaining capacity is the additional number of average virtual machines that can be deployed with the capacity that is available after the new virtual machines are sized. This is based on the fact that all required resources for provisioning machines should be available. So, if CPU capacity is available but memory or storage is not available, then the machines cannot be provisioned; thus all required resources are essential for provisioning virtual machines in the cloud environment.

The capacity management tool first calculates the remaining virtual machines based on each resource individually and then determines the remaining virtual machines based on the limiting resource.

 Remaining virtual machine CPUs = Remaining CPU capacity/CPU demand for an average virtual machine

 Remaining virtual machine memory = Remaining memory capacity/memory demand for an average virtual machine

The smaller of the two values provides the number of virtual machines that can be provisioned.

It is essential that capacity planning and the buying decisions of servers are based on a deep understanding and calculation of the above facts to utilize the compute resources to an optimum level. As an example, the newer servers with the new architecture support huge amounts of RAM on a single blade. Some of the servers support 384GB of RAM on a single blade. This provides for a greater number of virtual machines since RAM is not a limiting factor on these newer servers. However, if you ordered less RAM on your servers, you might run into issues of overcapacity on the CPU but no capacity in RAM, which would result in less optimal usage of the compute resources.

Virtual Environment Monitoring

Capacity monitoring has to be enabled for the whole cloud environment. The following four areas are important from monitoring perspective in a virtualized cloud environment:

- Virtual machines
- Hypervisor hosts
- DRS clusters
- Resource pool

Virtual machines

Virtual machine monitoring, as explained in the previous section, is about monitoring the utilization of the virtual machines CPU, memory, network, storage and IOPS. The granular monitoring of virtual machines provides the capacity for the overall cloud.

In addition to the virtual machine monitoring, the physical hosts that are used for the cloud infrastructure and the network components (including the external network, storage, and other features) need to be monitored for overall capacity, and performance thresholds must be configured so as to avoid any capacity-related incidents.

Key metrics to monitor and analyze are the following:

- CPU
- CPU usage
- CPU usage in MHz
- CPU used
- CPU ready
- CPU system
- CPU wait
- Disk
- Disk read rate
- Disk write rate
- Disk usage
- Disk read requests
- Disk write requests
- Memory
- Memory balloon
- Memory balloon target
- Memory usage
- Memory active
- Memory granted
- Memory consumed
- Memory swapped
- Network
- Network usage
- Network data transmit rate
- Network data receive rate

Hosts

In a virtual environment, the host represents the foundation, the core virtualization layer upon which all virtualized machines are built and operate. It is essential to monitor the hosts for any performance issues as these may impact the virtual machines running on it.

The key parameters are the following:

- CPU
- CPU usage
- CPU usage in MHz
- CPU used
- Disk
- Disk read rate
- Disk write rate
- Disk usage
- Disk read requests
- Disk write requests
- Memory
- Memory balloon
- Memory usage
- Memory active
- Memory granted
- Memory consumed
- Memory swapped used
- Memory shared common
- Network
- Network usage
- Network data transmit rate
- Network data receive rate

Distributed Resource Scheduler Clusters

DRS clusters are clusters that aggregate compute and memory resources from multiple physical servers into a single pool and make automated decisions to move virtual machines to different physical hosts based on the performance needs of the virtual machines. The DRS clusters need to be monitored for any performance degradation. Performance degradation issues within clusters could indicate underlying infrastructure problems in either the underlying host disk and/or network areas.

The following parameters need to be monitored:

- Cluster services
- Effective CPU resources
- Effective memory resources
- Current failover level

- CPU

- CPU usage in MHz

- Memory

- Memory balloon

- Memory usage

- Memory active

- Memory granted

- Memory shared common

- Memory swapped used

Resource Pools

Resource pools allow systems administrators to divide and allocate CPU and memory resources to virtual machines and other resource pools within a standalone host or DRS cluster. Resource pools aggregate the compute resources and allow administrators to provide limits, reservations, etc.

Using DRS clustering technology, the virtual platform can validate whether the underlying host infrastructure is able to meet the demand for the resource pool. If it is unable to service the demand appropriately, the platform will automatically attempt to allocate additional host resources within the DRS cluster to fulfill the requirements. In some cases, this could trigger a transparent, automated migration of virtual machines to another host or multiple hosts. In other cases, it could result in the temporary allocation of CPU and memory resources from the hypervisor host to the virtual machine.

The resource pools and DRS add another dimension to the capacity planning function and let administrators pool resources according to the types of applications and their compute usage. The following are the core metrics for resource pools:

- CPU

- CPU usage in MHz

- Memory

- Memory balloon

- Memory balloon target

- Memory usage

- Memory active

- Memory granted

- Memory consumed

- Memory swapped

Response Time Monitoring

The end-to-end response time monitoring from an end user's perspective is an important input into capacity management. Even after doing component capacity and ensuring that required capacity is available in all components, if the end user is unable to use the application because of performance issues, there will be dissatisfaction in the user community.

It is essential to use the outside-in monitoring tools to monitor applications using end user monitoring tools and provide appropriate response time for transactions from different locations. This will help in identifying core capacity issues or isolate issues in the networks from which end users are experiencing performance issues.

The end user monitoring can be done in the following ways:

- **Incorporating specific code within client and server applications software:** This can be used to provide complete end-to-end service response times or to provide a breakup of a transaction into its constituents.

- **Using synthetic scripts:** This provides an emulation of an end user using an application or system and can be repeated multiple times without the user actually using the application. This provides sample end-to-end service response times and is useful for providing representative response times. Note that this is not the actual time of the transaction as seen by a user, but it is the time seen by a synthetic or robotic user.

- **Distributed agent monitoring:** This is used to gauge the effect of location-specific variables on end-user monitoring. Agents are deployed in multiple locations and datacenters to gauge the response time of a system or application from diverse locations. This can be particularly helpful in finding and eliminating network related issues or other location specific issues.

Passive monitoring of network traffic is used to sniff the end user response time of applications or systems. This method relies on connecting specific network monitoring systems, often referred to as sniffers, inserted at appropriate points within the network. These systems record and monitor the network traffic and analyze this data to arrive at response times as it passes through each stage in the network.

The monitoring of response times is a complex process. It may use a combination of the above techniques and may leverage internal as well as external SaaS-based monitoring solutions. It is, however, essential and important that the monitoring service has high levels of availability and provides good service levels.

Alerts and Notification Management

There are several capacity management tools that gather capacity data from multiple sources, process and analyze the data using advanced statistics algorithms, and report on the results. These tools are capable of dynamically changing KPIs in terms of units of measurement in hours, minutes, or seconds; percentage increase or decrease in hardware, software, network; etc. Intelligent choice of tools and technologies for monitoring the cloud for capacity is essential for this capacity function.

The cloud resources are comprised of CPU, memory, network and disk I/O. This book explains the monitoring parameters and more; however, it is important that the alerting and notification system is fine-tuned to the cloud environment.

The following approach is recommended for the monitoring process:

- Identify the components of the cloud service.

- Create the health model for the cloud service.

- Identify the virtual machine monitoring parameters.

- Identify the host server monitoring parameters.

- Identify the storage parameters to be monitored.

- Identify the network parameters to be monitored.

- Develop thresholds for all components.

- Configure tools for auto baselining and throttling of unwanted events.

Key Considerations from Cloud Provider Perspective

The cloud provider is responsible for providing capacity on demand to the customers. For the cloud provider, excess capacity will mean waste, and less capacity than demand will mean loss of business. As compared to an enterprise leveraging owned data centers or an enterprise leveraging cloud services, the challenge and complexity for a cloud provider is much greater.

The cloud provider has to monitor the shared and supported infrastructure including the networks, storage, and hosts. Apart from this, the data on power consumption, ports, firewall ports, and load on shared services like load balancers is important from the cloud provider's perspective.

The cloud provider has to ensure that the service health model is created for the cloud service and that each component monitored for performance and analytics is used to provide capacity data and hot spots where there is a current or future chance of a bottleneck. A single component may become a bottleneck and render the complete cloud service unavailable.

Key Considerations from Cloud Consumer Perspective

The cloud consumer's primary monitoring aim is to ensure that the applications running on the cloud infrastructure are available and usable by the users within acceptable response times. Thus, the cloud consumer needs to monitor the response time of the application from the user's perspective. This may involve monitoring the application from various locations around the globe.

The cloud providers typically provide visibility to the cloud consumer on the performance data of their virtual machines. The cloud consumer needs to ensure that the monitoring data is consumed to provide details on capacity usage and trends. The cloud consumer can use automated means provided by the cloud provider or owner to make capacity addition decisions on runtime. This may include scaling up an application or scaling out an application. In scaling up, the application is scaled up to a higher configuration virtual machine; in scaling out, the application is instantiated on multiple servers.

Cloud computing frees the enterprises from monitoring the underlying infrastructure resources since the cloud provider provides this data in an on-demand model. The focus for the cloud consumer consuming infrastructure as a service cloud is more on ensuring the application performance and fine-tuning the applications.

CHAPTER 12

■ ■ ■

Capacity Analysis, Tuning, and Review

The monitoring systems, in cloud environments, carry out ongoing health checkups and keep generating monitoring data that requires in-depth analysis in order to derive meaningful information. This chapter explains the analysis of monitoring data and how this analysis helps in tuning the capacity in order to facilitate performance optimizations. Statistical algorithms are explained; these carry out the capacity analysis for trending and forecasting. The later parts of the chapter describe the capacity management review, which aims to improve the capacity management process itself. Key performance indicators (KPIs) are defined for the cloud capacity management process. The KPIs act as process performance metrics. Capacity reports that must be generated are also explained in this chapter.

Analysis

Analysis of monitored data is done via statistical toolsets that not only help identify capacity consumption trends but help predict future consumption. Analysis helps in the creation of capacity reports and tuning actions that make the cloud environment ready for future business needs. Analysis may include performing the activities in the following subsections.

Convert Data into Information Inputs for Modeling

Depending on the type of modeling being conducted, performance data from monitoring is translated into a form that can be used as an input to the model.

Performance Trending and Analysis at the Functional Level

Performance trends of data and their analysis are important for the functional owners of business applications. The functional owners can analyze the capacity reports and overlay this with the application architecture to arrive at capacity decisions or future updates required at the application tier.

Exception Trending and Analysis at the Functional Level

Exception data from the performance period is trended and analyzed by functional capacity owners (other trends are already produced by automated reporting). The functional expertise of the capacity owner is important in order to insure the quality of trending in this activity. Structured approaches like problem management techniques are adopted. See later sections of this chapter for the various statistical models used in this process.

Identification of Issues

At the functional tier, various issues are identified. This includes issues like improperly configured thresholds, consistent lack of capacity, incorrect configuration, unusual load patterns, etc. Some commonly known issues may include the following:

- Contention (data, file, memory, processor)
- Inappropriate distribution of the workload across available resources
- Inappropriate locking strategy
- Inefficiencies in the application design
- Unexpected increases in transaction rates
- Inefficient use of memory

Identification of Cost Reduction Opportunities

Cost reduction opportunities are analyzed and reported. Various techniques are used to analyze the cost reduction opportunities. These include modeling of various services, simulations, etc. The aim here is to provide optimized capacity to applications so that waste of capacity can be minimized and at the same time applications are provided the capacity that they need. Movement to a public cloud or private cloud platform can be one such cost reduction opportunity, which can be derived after the analysis of application patterns.

Validation by Inter-Functional Analysis

Identified issues and opportunities are discussed in an inter-functional meeting to validate any assumptions and cross-verify inferences drawn at the functional level. This includes different functions coming together and analyzing the capacity reports. This provides validation as well as fine-tuning of optimizations.

Tools and Data collection

Both agent-based and agent-less tools are used to monitor the virtual and cloud environments. These monitoring systems discover systems, collect detailed hardware and software inventory data, and gather key performance metrics required for capacity utilization analysis. The data collector should gather data from heterogeneous environments based on multiple platforms to do the following:

- Store the statistics in the database and build a performance history for each object.
- Collect and store inventory history for each object, such as a virtual machine move from one host to another. This is an important consideration in the cloud environment since the environment is dynamic, and applications and virtual machines can be provisioned based on need.

The toolset should consolidate data and events spanning multiple vendors, platforms, and sources. It should support agent-less and agent-based monitoring of the infrastructure, applications, real and synthetic end-user transactions, SNMP networks, configuration changes, business metrics, and custom information. It should collect data and events from other monitoring and event management tools. Toolset solutions should also monitor on-premise and public cloud resources (for example, storage, unified computing system (UCS)) and services such as SaaS, IaaS, and PaaS).

Analysis should include advanced algorithms that solve capacity optimization problems and should support analysis capabilities such as aggregation, trending, and benchmarking. Scenario modeling and what-if analyses help model and test various planning scenarios.

The end result of this analysis in a virtual environment should be *specific* and provide *actionable* information that enables capacity management to know the following:

- Where the current capacity constraints in memory, CPU, storage, and input or output are causing performance problems now (over the past 24 hours).

- Where (host, virtual memory, cluster, data center), when (in how many days), and why (root cause) future performance problems may develop.

- How to correctly size resources allocated to each virtual machine to achieve maximum performance with the least amount of hardware resources.

- Where to find unused virtual machines, snapshots, disk images, etc. in order to reclaim hardware resources.

- Resource consumption and cost allocation by applications and by departments.

- The number of "slots" that are available in each host, cluster, or resource pool for deploying new virtual machines.

The analytical toolset capability should include the following:

- Analysis of performance and workload by means of a wide range of analysis templates, such as heat maps and topology views imported from MS Visio.

- Analysis of resource utilization and workload to detect busiest periods, periodic behaviors, and baselines (for example, day profiles).

- Analysis of how operational and process events impact resource performance and workloads.

- Analysis of aggregated resources at different levels (such as physical cluster, logical grouping, etc.) and the ability to generate resource typical profiles (such as typical database instance profiles).

- Monitoring deviations from the baseline and a way to automatically notifying users.

- Analysis of how capacity needs are relate to business drivers by correlating resource performance with workloads.

Trending

The data collected from monitoring should be analyzed to identify trends from which the normal utilization and service levels, or baselines, can be established. By regular monitoring and comparison with this baseline, exception conditions in the utilization of individual components or service thresholds can be defined, and breaches or near misses in the SLAs can be reported and acted upon. Also, the data can be used to predict future resource usage or to monitor actual business growth against predicted growth.

Trending allows you to understand what is considered "normal," which serves as a benchmark to compare against any deviation from "normal." Any deviation from expected utilization levels, thresholds, or response times can be immediately detected and acted upon. (Thus, the trends you extrapolate from this analysis can also be highly relevant during the incident and problem management processes.)

These trends may be as granular as by hour or by day, because business workloads are not evenly distributed across the day or week. You may find such issues as bottlenecks, unbalanced workload distribution, inefficient use of memory, and more.

Figure 12-1 depicts the consumption trends of server CPU and memory at various hours in a day. This trend line helps to depict the high business activity in application layers during evening, which is reflected by the slope of the graph, circled in the figure, at corresponding hours.

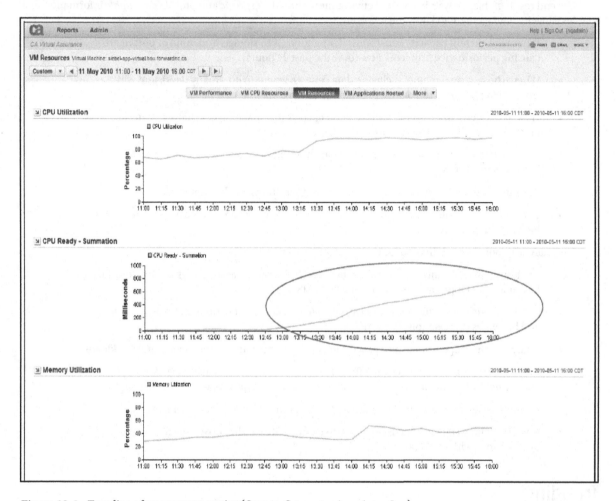

Figure 12-1. *Trending of server consumption (Source: Computer Associates, Inc.)*

Trend analysis is a measure to forecast future utilization needs with the help of historical data. An analysis of current system and component utilization may initiate efficiency improvements or the acquisition of additional IT components.

In cloud scenarios, the workload analysis and the variability in workload is an important factor. An application that has high variability becomes a good choice for the cloud to save on costs.

Forecasting

Forecasting activities allow the business to intelligently predict future growth and plan accordingly for capacity. This can be done in a variety of ways and we will discuss some algorithms or forecasting techniques.

Forecasting activities allow the business to intelligently predict future growth and plan accordingly for capacity. The low average utilization cost of servers is a well-known cost concern in data center management. Energy costs are rising, and low utilization translates into more physical machines, increasing expenditures for machine power and capital, and operational costs for cooling systems. Furthermore, excess machines require more floor space and added labor cost.

Low utilization has several causes. To guarantee good performance at periods of peak demand, processing capacity is over-provisioned for many business applications. However, processor demand typically exhibits strong daily variability leading to low average utilization. Another source of low utilization is the traditional deployment pattern of one application per OS image per unit of physical hardware.

In any case, after monitoring the daily or hourly utilization, you can find out the trends (peak demand period and low demand periods) and then control costs of low utilization by forecasting for the server utilization on different days or different hours. In a typical environment, a hypervisor executes on a physical machine and presents an abstraction of the underlying hardware to multiple virtual machines. After forecasting the resource utilization, you can do server consolidation, which can be static or dynamic. This is illustrated in Figure 12-2.

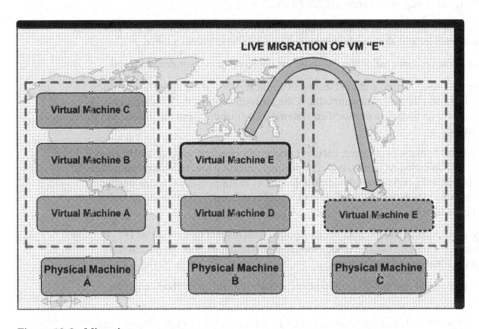

Figure 12-2. *Migration*

Three physical machines with a virtualization layer are used to execute five virtual machines. In the initial configuration, Physical Machine C can be in a low power state because it is not hosting any virtual machines. In response to demand change, Physical Machine C is activated and Physical Machine E is migrated from Physical Machine B to Physical Machine C. The migration occurs without service interruption. For migrations you must forecast utilization patterns accurately.

Modeling practices of cloud service providers must do the following:

- Ensure capacity modeling to balance the cost of capacity requirements against the benefits associated with business growth or service enhancement.

- Ensure tight integration with financial management to depict cost optimization options in terms of labor saving, reduced hardware capacity, and deferred capital expenditure.

- Deploy toolsets to optimize service performance and hardware spend by modeling the impact of a business change, such as increasing the number of customer orders, will have on performance and service response time.

- Deploy toolsets with a broad range of predictive capabilities, including correlation and analytic modeling, extrapolation analysis, and business "what-if" scenarios that support a proactive approach to prevent service disruptions and continuously align capacity with business demand.

- Ensure that the service provider deploys a toolset that can do the following:

  - Analyze how capacity needs are related to business drivers by correlating resource performance with business KPIs, such as identifying the storage space requirements of customer relationship management (CRM) users.

  - Estimate saturation points in terms of business metrics, such as identifying the maximum number of transactions that can be supported by the current infrastructure.

  - Provide flexible resource modeling components based on actual vendor platforms.

  - Facilitate modeling, sizing, and load testing of applications. For example, by providing flexible, user-friendly modeling capabilities, the tool will support the development of capacity criteria for a new or modified system being introduced to the production environment.

  - Model how infrastructure changes, such as horizontal or vertical scaling, and business changes, such as business trends, impact resource utilization and service response time. Identify bottlenecks and required additional capacity to support expected or desired growth in terms of business KPIs, while also respecting thresholds on resource utilization and response times.

  - Evaluate and compare different hardware options with respect to standards (TPC-C specification) or custom benchmarks, as well other criteria, such as overall cost or compliance with Green IT guidelines.

- Simulate how changes in cost models might affect accounting and chargeback analysis and reports.

- Ensure that component failure impact analysis, single point of failure, SPOF, FTA, and risk evaluation takes place. Ensure that future business requirements for IT services are quantified, designed, planned, and implemented in a timely fashion.

Statistical Models

There are various statistical models that can be used by the tools to provide capacity analysis. The statistical measures here utilize general approximations of the data collected by the technician for the analysis. These measures allow you to estimate trends or extrapolate to estimate future values. For these reasons, it is highly useful to use these techniques to gain the best estimates you can. Different statistical techniques are used for different purposes, and some may be better than others for a specific task. Let's start with a brief introduction to the most widely used statistical measures.

Time Series Analysis

Time series analysis is a useful technique to predict the performance of a system and calculate capacity requirements in the future based on past data.

A time series is a sequence of data points, measured typically at successive points in time spaced at uniform time intervals. The performance of a system's hourly averages plotted can be an input to the time series analysis. Time series are very frequently plotted via line charts.

Time series analysis comprises methods for analyzing time series data in order to extract the characteristics of the data. Time series forecasting is the use of a model to predict future values based on previously observed values.

Moving Average

IT forecasts demand by calculating an average of actual demand from a specified number of prior periods. Each new forecast drops the demand in the oldest period and replaces it with the demand in the most recent period; thus, the data in the calculation "moves" over time. As a result, in this model, the newer data points are more numerous than the older data points since the older data points are dropped from the calculation. This is well suited to scenarios where demand is changing over a period of time, so it is more reflective of the current situation.

The formula for a simple moving average is

$$A_t = \frac{D_t + D_{t-1} + D_{t-2} + \dots + D_{t-N+1}}{N}$$

where N = total number of periods in the average, D = the demand for a particular period. Thus the forecast for period t+1: $F_{t+1} = A_t$

Statistical algorithms play an important and integral part of the tools available for capacity planning. Forecasting toolset capability should include the following abilities:

- Estimate saturation dates (the dates of expected high volume) and residual capacity by using sophisticated algorithms. The tools use statistical analysis to arrive at the residual capacity.

- Estimate saturation points in terms of service or business metrics. This may include things like when the capacity for this particular infrastructure will be saturated. It should also have the ability to monitor forecasted capacity issues and automatically notify users

- Simulate infrastructural changes (horizontal or vertical scaling or failover) and business change scenarios (for example, business trends and marketing plans).

- Identify bottlenecks and required additional capacity to support the expected workload growth while respecting thresholds of resource utilization and response time (for example, SLAs).

- Compare different hardware options with respect to both standard and custom benchmarks and to other criteria, such as overall cost or compliance with GO GREEN guidelines.

- Simulate virtualization activities by identifying best candidates and targets and optimal placements with respect to technical, geographic, business, and compliance criteria.

- Simulate how a service scales from a test to production level environment by using load testing results.

- Account for resource consumption and charge cost back to the user as per the cost model.

- Allow users to access analysis and reports according to their roles through interactive dashboard views.

- Self-learn and adapt to the normal rhythmic behavior of IT components and business services over time.

- Forecast where the metrics may trend in the near future and how service may be impacted.

For example, VMware's vCenter Operations Manager uses statistical algorithms to capture and convert historical capacity usage data into trends to help visualize capacity usage patterns over time to forecast capacity use and availability. Trends are derived by fitting historical data into a trend curve. The trend curve is projected into the future to yield a forecast, as illustrated in Figure 12-3. The forecast horizon is the number of future intervals into which vCenter Operations Manager projects the trend.

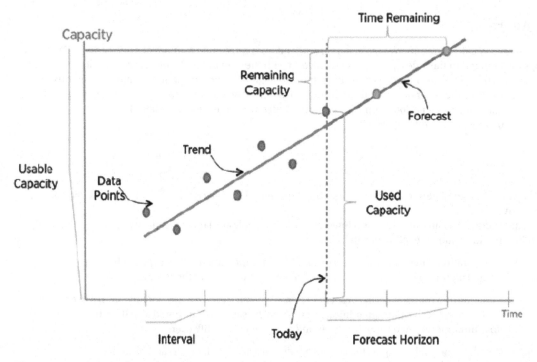

Figure 12-3. *VMware forecasting (Source: VMware)*

Most of the capacity forecasting tools use standard forecasting techniques. The accuracy of tool analysis is determined by how well the trend line matches the actual trend.

Tuning

Tuning helps better utilize system resources or improve the performance of a particular service by identifying steps to take that will optimize the system for current or anticipated workload. Tuning actions are primarily derived from analysis of capacity and performance data. Figure 12-4 describes a tuning procedure that uses the outcome of analysis procedure plus simulation and what-if analysis to finalize tuning actions. These actions, once approved, are implemented for ongoing capacity optimization.

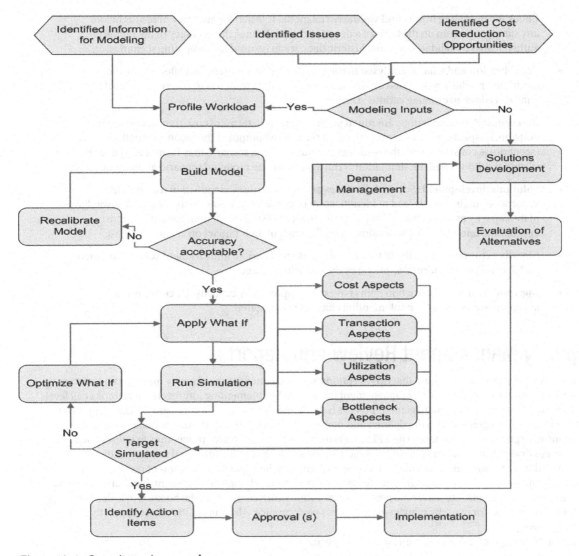

***Figure 12-4.** Capacity tuning procedure*

Performance tuning is the improvement of system performance. The motivation for such activity is called a performance problem, which can be real or anticipated. Most systems will respond to increased load with some degree of decreasing performance. A system's ability to accept a higher load is a significant element of *scalability*, and modifying a system to handle a higher load is in part a function of performance tuning.

The analysis of monitored data may identify areas of the configuration that could be tuned to better utilize the service, system, and component resources or improve the performance of the particular service. Tuning is an ongoing activity that ensures optimum resource utilization and performance actions are reviewed, modeled, and implemented. Tuning activity may include the following steps:

- **Profile workload:** This includes creating a holistic view of a workload, including dependencies, and mapping with other components of the cloud environment. There are discovery tools and procedures that help in establishing a workload profile. These tools automatically collect workload data including mappings with other components. These profiles are generally stored in a centralized database.

- **Check for modeling inputs and validate:** The model is tested for accuracy of results before any simulation is run on the basis of a developed model. Once the accuracy of the model is authenticated by validation against historic data, it can be used for simulating scenarios.

- **Recalibration and what-if analysis:** In case any inaccuracy is identified after testing the model, the model is redesigned on the basis of output data from test to correct it. What-if analysis is done to evaluate various scenarios.

- **Run simulation:** Simulations are run to predict impacts in terms of cost, transaction aspects, bottleneck aspects, utilization aspects, etc. If the desired output of the recommendation (scenario) is consistent with the results of a simulation, the scenario may be modified under certain conditions and the simulation is run again with the modified scenario as an input.

- **Solutions development:** Some of the issues and opportunities identified in the analysis subprocess might directly lead to identification of possible solutions on the basis of knowledge of the capacity environment. All possible solutions are listed for identification of the most appropriate one. Solutions are evaluated on the basis of their impact on service and cost.

- **Identify action items:** All the identified solutions and possible improvement actions are listed and documented for formal approval by the capacity manager.

- **Approvals:** All identified action items have to be approved by capacity. Once approved, appropriate processes for implementing changes are triggered.

Capacity Management Review and Reports

Capacity review is a critical procedure that drives continual improvement of the capacity management process by measuring performance of the capacity management process and implementing improvement actions at all levels.

To ensure that the capacity management process is working efficiently and is constantly seeking optimization actions, capacity management KPIs are defined and monitored. These KPIs act as process hooks to measure procedure-wise process performance. The KPI reports must feed into respective procedures to help capacity management design and architect capacity management processes as per business and service needs.

In addition, these KPIs must include all the aspects related to the capacity management process, including process dependencies on event management, demand management, change management, incident management, configuration management, etc. There must be integrated KPIs with management dashboards in order to provide a high level of visibility for capacity management process performance. Also these KPIs must support dynamic reporting views.

Capacity management KPIs must include the following:

- Production of workload forecasts on time

- Percentage of accuracy of forecasts of business trends

- Increased ability to monitor performance and throughput of all services and components

- Accurate forecasts of planned expenditures

- Percentage reduction in the number of incidents due to poor performance

- All new services implemented matching SLRs

- Timely incorporation of business plans into the capacity plan

- A number of agreed-upon SLAs and operational level agreements (OLAs) with performance metrics

- Percent of SLA and OLA performance metrics that can be proactively maintained through automatic resource provisioning

- Percent of IT resource usage covered by SLA and OLA with performance metrics

- Customer satisfaction with SLA and OLA performance parameters and attainment

- Percent of SLA and OLA performance parameters attained

- Percent of SLA and OLA performance parameters clearly prioritized based on the value of the service or agreement

- Value of SLA and OLA performance parameters attained vs. not attained

- Accurate forecasts of planned expenditure

- Number of inaccurate business forecast inputs provided

- Total dollars in unused capacity expenditures

- Percentage of capacity forecasts that were accurate

- Timely justification and implementation of new technology in line with business requirements (time, cost, and functionality)

Capacity Reports

Capacity management reporting must happen at different layers for different stakeholders in order to facilitate decision making and make capacity management truly cost justifiable. Capacity management reports must be prepared and shared with stake holders to facilitate decision making. As discussed earlier, capacity reporting has to be done at various layers, and an aggregated view of the capacity available on the cloud should be the outcome.

Furthermore, reports must be produced for distinct audiences, such as

- **The business:** Is it really focused on delivery to time and budget?

- **IT management:** Management will be interested in the tactical and strategic results that support the business.

- **IT operational or technical managers:** These people will be concerned with the tactical and operational metrics that support better planning, coordination, and scheduling of resources. The operational managers will be interested in their technology domain measurements such as component availability and performance.

Reporting procedures also must be able to present reports via the medium of choice: web-enabled dynamic HTML, current snapshot whiteboards, or real-time portal or dashboards.

Capacity management performance is tracked and monitored based on SLAs and service improvements are initiated. IT process KPIs are linked with business metrics for "service down" reporting; this is fully integrated with the Continual Service Improvement (CSI) process. There must be a provision for flexible report generation and production of management reports from historical service level records. These reports and improvement actions must feed into the CSI process.

The important reports from overall cloud capacity are as follows:

- Overall cloud capacity available

- Overall cloud capacity used

- Overall cloud capacity unused

- Forecast report for cloud capacity available/used

- Forecast for demand

- Datacenter-wise/location-wise reports

- Cluster-wise/resource pool-wise reports

- Under-utilized/over-utilized forecast

- Yield per cloud unit

- Capacity usage by types of virtual machines

The metrics of each section are as follows:

- Details of cloud service cloud service capacities:

  - Agreed capacities

  - Measured capacity usage

- Details of service performance:

  - Agreed performance

  - Measured performance

- Trend analysis components:

  - Expected increase or decrease in demand for service capacities

  - Threshold values, the attainment of which triggers the start of measures for the expansion of service capacities

- Incidents leading to reduced service capacities or performance:

  - In the past (prolonged service failures, etc.)

  - Type of incident

  - Causes

  - Countermeasures for elimination of failure

  - Measures for future avoidance of similar failures

  - In the future (i.e., planned prolonged downtimes to services)

- Analysis of effects upon IT capacities by

  - Changes, additions, or cancellations of IT services

  - Forthcoming changes

  - New technologies

  - External changes, such as of a judicial type

Capacity management staffing

For any organization to achieve optimum staffing, the capacity management process should be sufficiently staffed in order to address the immediate needs or customer issues related to poor performance coming from insufficient capacity. Roles like capacity manager, capacity and performance analyst, etc. must be clearly defined. In addition, an organization's staffing and resources should be optimized and continuously evaluated to ensure their most efficient use.

To ensure appropriate cost justified staffing, the following actions must be adopted by cloud service providers:

- Base workload predictions on operational data to deduce inputs from them for capacity planning procedures as well.

- Periodically perform modeling and workload forecasting in order to keep an eye on optimum staffing requirements.

- Procure skills for specific activities where the required skills are not available internally or where it is more cost-efficient to do so.

- As a high level of automation is already in place, ensure optimum staffing levels to carry out manual assignments or tasks that cannot be automated like compliance checks, approvals, and critical decision making.

- Ensure that staffing requirements are provided adequately in order to ensure the agreed quality of live IT service levels.

- Document the skills that exist in the organization along with those that need to be developed in order to identify current skill inventories. Required skills can be identified through interviews, group discussions, questionnaires, and performance feedback of the resources.

- Adequately staff critical resources like technical analysts or architects, technical managers, IT operations manager, etc.

- Examine tasks that are repeatable in nature for potential automation to reduce cost, effort, and potential errors.

- Ensure that workload balancing and staffing are driven by identifying automation opportunities.

- Focus on resource reduction of repetitive automatable jobs.

- Deploy processes to continuously evaluate activities and automation opportunities.

■ ■ ■

CHAPTER 13

Capacity Management Database and Integrations

This section of the book describes the need and role of the capacity management database. The capacity database forms the repository of all capacity-related information. The capacity plan also resides in the capacity database. The concept of a managed object is introduced here for cloud providers. Managed objects are the representation of technical objects that contribute to delivering cloud services. This chapter also explains detailed input/output aspects of the capacity management process with regard to other IT service management processes, CMDB, monitoring systems, and other data center databases. The definition and type of data that must reside in capacity databases is also discussed. Finally, this chapter emphasizes capacity database and CMDB integration.

Configuration Management Database and Capacity Database

In a cloud environment, managed objects become more important for the aggregator and deliverer roles, and OMDBs (object management databases) are the central focus. A managed object is an abstracted representation of technical infrastructure as seen by and for the purpose of management. These managed objects can be virtual instances running in a cloud environment and are comprised of virtual servers, virtual storage, virtual networks, etc.

Each of the capacity management subprocesses generates and uses any of the types of data stored in the capacity database (CDB). The core infrastructure record, the CMDB, provides information about the state of assets and the relationships among assets. By providing performance and resource information about the CIs of the CMDB, a CDB works in tight synergy with the CMDB to provide a complete, reliable, and robust view of the business or IT infrastructure, including information about the business, service, technical, financial, and utilization data. These views provide a service item view of cloud infrastructures. A service may be supported by a group of CIs including network, storage, memory, and CPUs. The service mapping of individual CIs with service items ensures discovery procedures at the CMDB level. This helps to catch service mapping trends and information from the capacity database. These trends and analysis reports can be readily viewed through reporting dashboards. Financial models also may leverage this service mapping matrix for charging and accounting activities. Financial data becomes important in the cloud world for calculating total cost of ownership (TCO).

Figure 13-1 provides details on how the capacity database interacts with various processes. CDB becomes a subset of a federated CMDB, with common access to CIs that permits access to the data from all interested consumers.

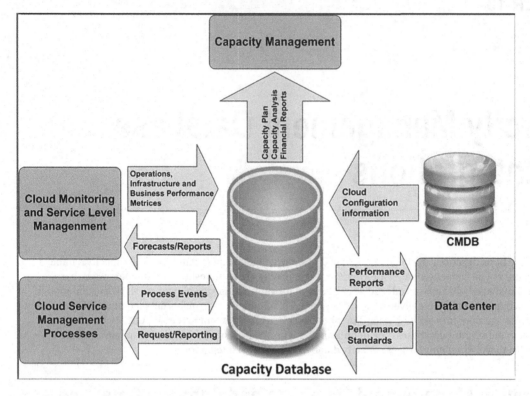

Figure 13-1. *Capacity database input/outputs*

The CMDB record includes the following:

- Name of the instance

- Expiration information

- OS of the instance

- Primary IP address associated with the instance

- The secondary IP addresses associated with the instance

- Server size of the instance

- Storage disk size of the instance

- Host name of the instance

- Image from which the instance has been created

- Date of creation of the instance

- Status of the instance

- Originator that requested the instance

- Price charged for the instance per UHR

- Running time elapsed since the instance has been provisioned (in hours)
- Instance tags
- Notifications about the instance event

Data Type Description

In this section we will give a quick description of the following data types:

- Business Data
- Service Data
- Technical Data
- Financial Data
- Utilization Data

Business Data

Business data includes the number of users of an application, number of PCs, number of accounts, number of products supported, and/or the number of web site business transactions executed.

Service Data

Service data represents the effect that the IT infrastructure has on the work of the end user. As such, this includes batch turnaround times or online response times. It is useful to include performance threshold data with service data to represent the SLAs that service level management and capacity management have agreed to.

Technical Data

Technical data represents the component limits in the infrastructure. It helps determine, for each entity, the point where over-utilization degrades performance of business services. ITIL limits technical data to this construct, but acknowledges that actual thresholds depend on the kind of work being executed. For example, a server may be limited to running at only 40 percent utilization due to input or output constraints. Ideally, the component limits are sensitive to the work being executed.

Financial Data

Financial data includes a variety of information regarding costs. Some of the items in the following list are not part of the CDB, but instead link to sources where the financial data that is to be stored in the CDB can be obtained:

- Financial costs of upgrades
- Cost of maintaining the current hardware
- Revenue gained by the organization through processing a transaction
- Costs associated with processing a transaction

Often, a valuable use of the data in the CDB is to develop the chargeback costs—what the IT organization charges for services provided. This enables the business to weigh revenue against the cost of doing business.

Utilization Data

Utilization data reports utilization numbers, including current and historical values. Part of the management of a CDB includes automation of data collection, summarization, and archiving. Though many options exist, an ideal option is one where system metrics map directly to business workloads and applications, thus expanding the value of the data beyond the IT organization.

Integration of the Capacity Database with the Configuration Management Database

The following three types of data from a CMDB can be useful for capacity planning purposes (for creating analysis and what-if scenarios):

- CI properties such as asset information (the hardware details and configuration properties)

- CI relationships describing service structures and topologies

- Services defined in the service catalog

CDB should make it easy to import these three types of data from a CMDB. Capacity management should have an open and extensible CDB. Capacity management should provide standard (out-of-the-box) connectors to the major CMDBs, in particular to an integrated CMDB. Data in the form of XML files can be exported to access CMDB data

The cloud service provider must deploy automated toolsets for collection and aggregation of component and system data to measure capacity and performance levels of IT services (for example, e-mail services and payroll services). This data must reside in the CDB with service-to-CI view options, etc.

Also, the toolset that facilitates the recording of all relevant capacity data in a repository must be implemented (for example, the ability to store service, system, and component utilization data for reporting and analysis purposes).

Other toolset capabilities must include the following:

- Drill-down capabilities to users, CIs, and processes active at the time of a performance problem.

- Features to ensure that the toolset facilitates application sizing, such as building a system model including all required technology components to estimate resource requirements for a new or changed service.

- Options to facilitate the identification of workload and usage patterns over time.

- Access to historic and time-defined capacity and performance data in order to facilitate trend analysis in a graphical format, such as graphical illustrations of patterns of business activity.

- Interfaces with statistical calculation and summarization tools (for example, Statistical Package for the Social Sciences (SPSS), etc.)

- The ability to predict process, transaction, and job response times based on system loads and volumes.

- Providing workload and queue result statistics, both summarized and in detail.

Integration Approach

The integration approach provides details on how the integration of processes, CMDB, and CDB is done to provide the needed inputs for a robust capacity management process.

- The first step involves replacing the current (automated) integration of configuration data from monitoring tools.

- The second step integrates additional information about the service catalog and the service structure (the relationships among the CIs).

- The third step creates processes to automatically activate capacity planning activities (for example, analyses and reports) on newly deployed services and components.

Benefits

The benefits of an integrated capacity management process with CMDB and CDB with all required data are the following:

- **Cost reduction:** Timely ("just-in-time") provisioning enables savings on both resource and operational costs.

- **Operational efficiency:** Integration with other IT service management processes and tools enables better Runbook Automation (RBA).

- **Risk avoidance:** Automated capacity planning of newly delivered CIs and services improves service availability and guarantees higher levels of service.

Capacity Management Tools Integration

One of the prime success factors in designing any capacity solution resides in its integration capabilities with other systems that are running in a cloud environment. These may be orchestrators, self-service portals, ITSM tools, etc. As discusses in earlier chapters, capacity solutions must be able to easily monitor, gather, analyze, and report on capacity-related data from multiple sources. Some of the known integrated capacity management solutions are provided by vendors like Netuitive, CiBRA, BMC, VMware, and CA. These management tools help in achieving high levels of automation in all capacity management activities.

Capacity management tools must ensure the integration with other systems, as mentioned in Figure 13-2.

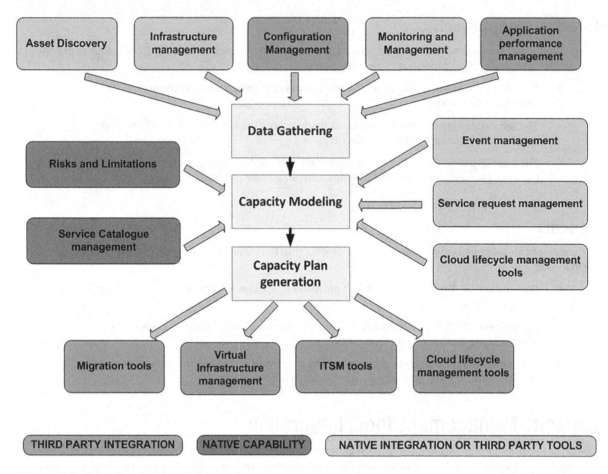

Figure 13-2. Capacity solution tools integration

These integration tools may primarily include

- Physical-to-virtual migration tools
- Configuration management tools
- Discovery tools
- Cloud orchestrators
- Cloud lifecycle management/self service portals
- ITSM ticketing tools
- Event management systems
- Chargeback/showback tools
- Reporting tools

Capacity Management Process Relations

No process can create business efficiencies and desired process outcomes when it functions in silo. To serve the purpose of economies, efficiency, and effectiveness, all process areas must be integrated and closely coupled. This is greatly supported by automation and ITSM integration. Though there are several process areas that must be in line with capacity management, the following subsections outline the prime ITSM processes that must be integrated with capacity management to ensure business aligned IT.

Demand Management

Demand management process dependencies and coupling has already been mentioned in earlier sections.

Demand data is an essential input to a robust and mature capacity management process. Demand data is a key input to predict future capacity needs and make decisions on capacity placement and leveraging cloud services.

Demand management provides patterns of business activities that are then translated to service and component capacity. Demand management also provides anticipated service levels for which capacity must be allocated in advance.

Capacity demand coupling is one of the prime areas for capacity management. Capacity management helps demand management in creating service packages by providing reports on capacity, and demand management in turn provides demand forecasts and patterns to capacity management for effective capacity planning.

IT service Continutity Management

IT service continuity processes provide the service continuity plan as an input to the capacity management process. This includes the service continuity measures, DR plans, and details on ensuring continuity. This data is essential for capacity planning as DR and service continuity process demands need to be met through capacity planning.

The cloud is emerging as a good option for various organizations to host their DR in. Cloud providers provide DR facilities for their cloud service. Most providers also have multiple regions or locations across which the customer can deploy an application to provide for DR scenarios.

The service continuity process provides the report on business impact analysis, which is shared with capacity management in order to take necessary actions for capacity planning. The capacity management process provides optimum capacity requirements to support IT service continuity planning.

Release Management

The capacity management process ensures that during releases adequate capacity is available for new and changed services. The release management process provides the details on capacity needs of new or changed services to the capacity management process. Release management provides release notifications to capacity management for performance monitoring and capacity planning.

Availability Management

The capacity management process and plans are used by the availability management process for availability planning. Performance monitoring reports on capacity management are shared with the availability management team to assist in ensuring committed availability.

Availability management provides the details on availability requirements, which are an input to capacity planning. As an example, a highly available application may need two or more instances running or a standby machine, which may increase the need for capacity. In the cloud model, high availability considerations can increase the cost of the infrastructure since multiple instances or storage may be needed to provide for higher availability.

Service Level Management

The capacity management process assists service level management processes for agreed SLAs, OLAs, and UCs. The service level management process provides SLA targets, SLR targets to capacity management for designing capacity, and forms the basis for capacity performance reporting.

This is a key input to capacity planning. The service levels determine the capacity requirements.

This is also a key parameter to look at before migrating to the cloud. Since SLAs from various cloud providers vary hugely, it is important to read through and decipher the SLAs provided by the cloud providers and the conditions attached.

Financial Management

Capacity management provides information and data for cost calculations, budgeting, and charging. In return, financial management provides the budgets and calculated costs for fulfilling capacity requirements and reports on actual costs.

This aspect is also a key consideration before making a decision to move to cloud. The Opex vs. Capex calculations need to be done, and ROI for any workload movement to the cloud needs to be in place.

CHAPTER 14

Capacity Management Concepts

This chapter introduces the latest trends in capacity management that enable cloud providers to perform capacity management with the highest level of maturity. These trends include predictive trends in capacity calculations, while self learning systems add intelligence, automation, and accuracy. Concepts like yield management help service providers in selling the right capacity with the right resources. Further, trends like VM sprawl management are discussed in this chapter. VM sprawl is one of the areas of concern in virtualized environments.

Threshold Management

Service level breaches and performance degradation are primarily governed and detected through monitoring toolsets. These toolsets use the service breach limits popularly known as *thresholds*. These thresholds set the guidance for subsequent alerting and notification actions. Threshold monitoring tools throw alerts that can be classified on the basis of criticality and impact. Note that utter care must be taken while setting thresholds. Many thresholds are dependent on the task that is being executed on a particular component.

Thus it becomes critical to manage thresholds, as this plays a key role in delivering services with desired performance and service levels. Setting thresholds at appropriate levels ensures the effectiveness of alerts and notifications that are generated when a service breach happens or is about to happen. These notifications help in performing remedial actions for service continuity and maintaining the agreed service levels. There are toolsets available that intelligently determine the probability of threshold breaches. In addition, these toolsets use behavior analytics to establish the threshold breach patterns and automatically set new threshold limits. These toolsets are also capable of diagnosing false alerts that monitoring tools produce.

Besides this, at times there is a need to optimize dynamic cloud environments, which may include workload movement across heterogeneous environments, such as workload movement within hybrid clouds when optimization of cloud components and resources is needed to maintain or improve performance or throughput. This is achieved using workload management tools and techniques like DRS, vMotion, etc., as described earlier. This movement causes implications for automatic threshold management due to the dynamic nature of the workloads and underlying infrastructure.

Emerging Trends in Capacity Management

The following subsections outline emerging trends in capacity management.

Self-Learning Capability

Heuristics and behavioral analysis have been used in the IT security realm for years. Real-time behavioral analysis provides the same benefit of self-learning anomaly detection in the data center. Rather than trying to model constantly changing performance variables, performance management should analyze behavior in real time and correlate infrastructure performance quickly into application performance and vice versa.

Automated Threshold Management

As part of the self-learning capability, thresholds should be adaptive. Performance management tools for a virtual environment should be able to learn and build behavior profiles for servers, virtual machines, and applications, and also adapt thresholds for changing behavior.

Visibility into Individual Virtual Machine and System Behavior

There are so many moving parts of a virtual infrastructure that it can be nearly impossible to isolate the cause of an application performance issue. It's critical to have visibility into the health of each virtual machine and the health of the overall system. It is also important to have multiple contexts, such as knowing the relative performance of a virtual machine to its host hypervisor server as well as the entire pool of resources.

Today there are specialized, modern, capacity management solution providers in self-learning analytics for performance and capacity management. These capacity and performance management solutions work across discrete cloud environments to provide end-to-end visibility, automated problem diagnostics, and predictive analytics. Figure 14-1 describes a self-learning solution that is capable of providing a next-generation capacity management solution that can identify and proactively rectifying capacity-related issues even before occurrence.

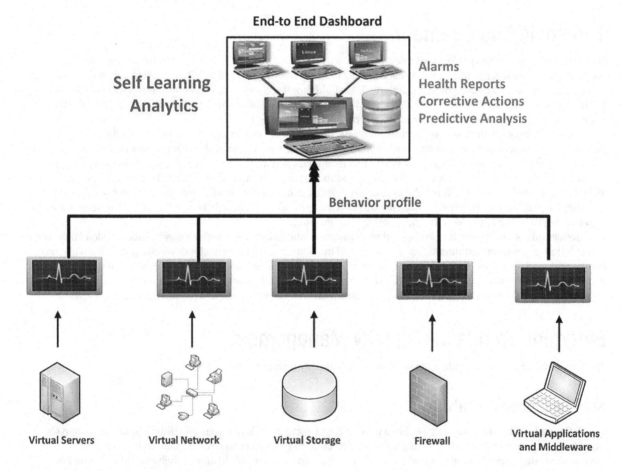

Figure 14-1. Self-learning capacity solutions

Proactive Capacity Planning

Performance management tools need to offer resource allocation and capacity planning before deployment as well as in production. The value of virtualization is flexibility and resource optimization. Tools that can deliver that optimization from the onset are the most valuable.

Yield Management

"Selling the right capacity to the right customer at the right price"

Yield management is not the latest technique for capacity planning and pricing. Initially adopted by service providers in airlines, trains, and buses as a profit maximization strategy, yield management works on the principles of over-purchase, pricing, and capacity allocation.

One of the greatest challenges in running an infrastructure-as-a-service cloud is how to establish the trade-off between performance delivery and cost effectiveness. The key metric behind this is the hardware utilization rate used in the cloud; too high and performance suffers, too low and prices inevitably rise. Yield management perfectly answers this question of how a cloud provider should deliver performance and value for the money.

Recently this technique has been effectively adopted by cloud service providers to help them decide how to maximize the utilization of resources and ensure value for the money. For example, cloud service providers need to know how much of each type of virtual machine (whether it be small, medium, or large in a virtual machines profile) to allocate to different types of customer demand with flexible pricing models.

Yield management in cloud capacity management can achieve several objectives, including the following:

- Improving the ability to anticipate virtual resource demand and allocate capacity effectively and efficiently

- Maximizing capacity utilization of virtual resources

- Optimizing pricing to maximize revenue and manage demand

- Managing customer expectations with regard to service level and resource performance

- Establishing the trade-off between price and performance

Figure 14-2 describes the trade-off between cost and performance in order to meet future demand while having optimum resource utilization and cost effectiveness.

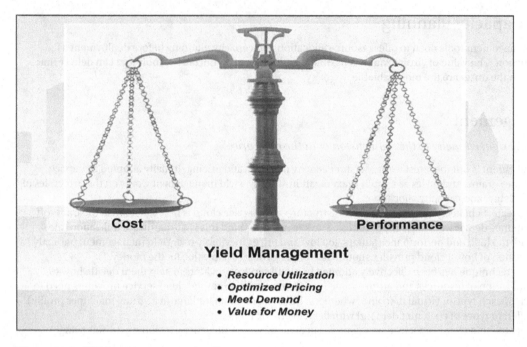

Figure 14-2. *Yield management trade-off*

The various models in which cloud capacity are sold today are as follows:

- **Long-Term Contracts:** Wherein the customer buys capacity for a fixed long-term duration. In this model, a discount is offered for the on-demand pricing since there is surety of business and a consistent requirement from the customer over a fixed contract. This is akin to the hosting model that has been prevalent for so long.

- **On-Demand Compute:** Here the customers are typically charged on a per-hour basis; however, in this model the cloud vendor can see huge fluctuations in demand since customers may be using hybrid clouds and may burst into the cloud infrastructure for extra compute needs. The cloud vendor can use yield optimization techniques in this model where the customers can be incentivized for compute capacity utilization on the basis of availability of compute capacity at a point in time. This could be achieved using a notification mechanism wherein the current pricing, adjusted for availability of capacity, is published and the demand and supply mechanism takes care of the optimum yield of the cloud capacity. This is similar to the *spot pricing model* wherein people can subscribe to the service to gather information on the pricing and bid on the spot instances to reserve their instances. However, in this model, the moment the consumer is outbid they run the risk of losing their instances. The decisions on over-provisioning the capacity have to be also taken into account, keeping in mind the utilization trends of various users, customers, and hosts.

These concepts can take the form of a multi-cloud market wherein the buyers and sellers bid or reverse bid for capacity. A reverse bidding mechanism in cloud computing can get users the capacity at cheap prices and also give maximum yield to the cloud provider.

VM Sprawl Management

Implementing a private cloud makes it easier for development, test resources, and application deployment resources to order virtual machines. After a while, the enterprise will see virtual machines sprawled all over, consuming processing power and storage even though they are not being used.

VM sprawl is an unwanted side effect of the easy and fast provisioning process. VM sprawl can become a huge problem and negate the benefits of implementing a private cloud.

The solution to the VM sprawl problem is to implement the following:

- Organizational awareness and training resources on the usage of virtual machines and the cloud infrastructure.

- Capacity reports that flag over-utilized, under-utilized, and not utilized machines, and define a time after which an automatic process will be initiated to reclaim the unused machines.

- Chargebacks to ensure that costs are allocated to departments using the cloud infrastructure and thus ensuring that users surrender unused virtual machines.

■ ■ ■

Capacity Plan Template

The following is a section-by-section overview of what should be included in a capacity plan. So this is in essence a template for a capacity plan.

A capacity plan is used to manage the resources required to deliver IT services. The plan contains scenarios for different predictions of business demand and cost options to deliver the agreed service level targets.

The purpose of the capacity plan described and templated below is to help formulate the strategy for assessing and managing infrastructure component performance. The information populated in a capacity plan facilitates the capacity planning decisions. These decisions may include additional infrastructure acquisition, configuration changes, and upgrading decisions to meet business requirements efficiently.

Planning for capacity ensures that the business requirements are efficiently and effectively met by the infrastructure and application elements of the solution. It provides management with the following:

- A clear understanding of current resource capacities to support the business solutions

- An assessment of current capacity management capacities

- A list of resources to be included or upgraded to meet future business demand

Document Control

In a capacity plan, it is necessary to create a working system of document controls. As the plan progresses, the stages the plan goes through change and so does the plan document. It is not surprising that there are commonly-used terms for the various stages the capacity plan passes through. Document status includes the following stages:

- **Drafts:** These are documents for review and liable to have significant changes.

- **Working Baseline:** The document has reached the end of the initial review phase and can be used as the basis for technical design, but is expected to have further changes. This document will have changes tracked since the last draft.

- **Baseline Candidate:** The document is ready for final issuing and is only expected to have further minor updates.

- **Baseline:** The document is published and is not expected to change. This document will have changes tracked since the working baseline.

Now let's look at capacity plan ingredients and what should be included under each section. Please note that this plan is based on the best practices as specified by leading technology providers and frameworks like ITIL. You can certainly have an organization-specific capacity plan in this dynamic and ever-changing IT environment. The remainder of this appendix is the actual capacity plan template.

Executive Summary

Much of the capacity plan, by necessity, contains technical detail that is not of interest to all readers of the plan. The executive summary section should highlight the main issues, options, recommendations, and costs. It should also contain the main points from each of the sections of the main plan. The prime goal of the document is to provoke investment decisions for the right areas and to avoid or postpone investment decisions where appropriate. Therefore, this section should cut straight to the main business issues to be addressed and decisions needed—remembering that a decision to take no action is still a key decision.

Avoid any technology detail not essential to the decision. State the issues having the most business impact, the cost options, and briefly any justifiable recommendations.

The overall capacity and performance plan is likely to contain many recommended investments and complex financial analysis, so the executive summary of the overall infrastructure capacity and performance plan may be spun off into a separate document and may focus on specific financial and business-based readerships.

Introduction

A capacity plan supports the goal of optimum, and cost effective, provisioning of organizational resources and services by matching them to business demands. The capacity plan reflects the current and future needs of the business. It helps identify and reduce inefficiencies associated with either under-utilized resources or unmet customer demand and to provide for satisfactory service levels in a cost-efficient manner. The plan helps ensure that all infrastructure components are capable of performing all required functions, and that those components will perform as efficiently as possible and can accommodate reasonable growth without being overly wasteful.

This section should contain summary information on the following:

- The time scope of the plan (whether this is an annual, six-month, or rolling monthly plan)

- The components, services, facilities, resources, and skills within the scope of this plan

- The current levels of capacity

- The current performance delivered, including service level achievements and information on the performance incidents logged

- A summary of incidents caused by under-capacity

- A view on when service incidents or financial impact are envisaged due to over- or under-capacity

- Changes in the infrastructure, business environment, plans, and forecasts since the last issue of the plan

Scope and Terms of Reference of the Plan

This section of the plan should consider the aims, objectives, and deliverables, plus the wider issues of people, processes, tools, and techniques. It should encompass all IT resources.

For example, the capacity plan should cover details of the following:

- Business capacity management (translates business needs and plans into requirements for service and IT infrastructure)

- Service capacity management (the management, control, and prediction of the end-to-end performance and capacity of the live operational IT services usage and workloads)

- Component capacity management (the management, control, and prediction of the performance, utilization, and capacity of individual IT technology components)

This section should explicitly name elements of the above that are included and those that are excluded.

Methods Used

Capacity management is highly dependent on information provided by other processes. This section should state the sources of information, the tools used to gather and analyze information, and the methods used to model the impact on the infrastructure and service performance. This is likely to include monitoring data from infrastructure components, application performance tools, business forecasts (including macro-economic impacts), workload forecasts, modeling techniques, and the output from service modeling tools.

This should include performance, availability, and service level data normally produced by existing monitoring tools that investigate infrastructure components and application execution, producing detailed workload forecasts and statistics on end user delivery. More mature organizations will also include business forecasts (including macro-economic impacts), modeling techniques used, and the output from service modeling tools.

Application

This must include the data regarding each of the organization's applications and document them. It must also be ensured that all applications have been accounted for and information regarding each application is correct.

Infrastructure

This section includes data regarding the data center's virtual and physical assets and documents them within this workbook. All devices must be accounted for and information regarding each device must be correct. This section translates the forecasted services demand into utilization of infrastructure resources (such as processor, memory, storage, licenses, network, data center, and power). A best practice is to use service capacity models to make these calculations. Investment in capacity tools can be highly effective in improving the quality of the resource demand analysis and the visual impact of the material.

Gathering the data necessary to write this section will entail closely working with the infrastructure and monitoring technical staff. Close cooperation in this effort among the various technical teams will often yield insights in how to make better use of the existing investment to obtain better data and better performance.

This section should show the recent utilization across all the infrastructure towers and also forecast resource demand at least 12 months ahead. Any critical dates where infrastructure constraints would produce performance incidents or outages should be highlighted. The options and recommendations sections should contain suggestions for avoidance of the negative business impact.

User Task Scenarios

Usage scenarios (also called use cases) define the sequences of tasks users perform and their interactions with solution functions to help them to perform the tasks. This section of capacity plan should define the scenarios that are worked upon by users in their respective functional areas. Identifying and describing usage scenarios provides details that enable the estimation of capacity loads and other factors.

Task Load Matrix

The task-load matrix describes the different kinds of load that each usage scenario puts on the system. This matrix measures for both server and client configurations as appropriate to the capacity-planning scenario.

Monitoring and Metrics

The monitoring and metrics section describes the monitoring methods, techniques, and tools that will be used to evaluate solution and component performance, and provides metrics for planning intervention. This information should be provided for each major component at the solution level.

Service Demand and Forecasts

Business plans should provide capacity management with details of the new services planned and the growth or contraction in the use of existing services. This subsection should report on new services and the demise of legacy systems. This section should profile the IT services provided in terms familiar to the service managers and business leaders (such as service transaction peaks, mean and total, number of accounts processed, and so on). Profiles and forecasts should be provided for new and existing services, including any plans for service retirement. Short-term, mid-term, and long-term forecasts should be included based on the best information available from business plans, promotion, and activity schedules. Critical and high-impact business services should be profiled individually, while less-critical services may be aggregated, provided this still permits the resource demand to be estimated.

Service Tiers

These tiers are used to ensure that appropriate service tiers like Gold, Bronze, and Silver are based on a pre-established set of application criticality criteria

Third Party

This section collects all contact information from vendors and internal contacts so that it is readily available to all stakeholders. Once drafted, the capacity plan is circulated among all stakeholders in a non-ambiguous and accessible format presenting component, service, and business views for implementation in ongoing capacity management.

User Profile

User profiles describe users of a proposed solution and certain important user characteristics such as frequency of solution use and competence in using a solution. Users can be identified in groups (or classes), usually stated in terms of their functional areas. Information technology users include help desk, database administration, etc. Business users include accounting, warehousing, procurement, etc. Describing the users and their important characteristics assists in forming scenarios that are relevant to capacity.

Usage Scenarios

Usage scenarios (also called use cases) define the sequences of tasks users perform and their interactions with solution functions to help them to perform the tasks. This section should define the scenarios performed by the users in each functional area. Identifying and describing usage scenarios provides details that enable the estimation of capacity loads and other factors.

Scenario 1 <<Scenario description>>

This section describes a scenario and its characteristics that provide input to estimating loads, growth, and impacts.

Scenario 2 <<Scenario description>>

Task-load Matrix

This section describes what load capacity components bear in order to execute the user tasks. Table A-1 measures for both server and client configurations as appropriate to the capacity-planning scenario.

Table A-1. *Load Capacity for Server and Client Configurations*

Scenario Load	User Scenario 1	User Scenario 2	User Scenario 3	User Scenario 4	User Scenario 5
Storage					
Software					
CPU					
Memory					
I/O					
Others					

Expected Growth

The expected growth table (Table A-2) describes the growth pattern for the scenarios as a function of time.

Table A-2. *Expected Growth*

Capacity Type	Current Capacity Analysis	Planned/Expected Growth and Recommendations
Describe the capacity scenario analyzed. Enter details on current and future capacity requirements.	Describe currently available capacity.	Describe how future growth expectations have been identified and analyzed. Outline recommendations for managing and addressing this expected growth.

Assumptions Made

Modeling errors are less common than failures in the assumptions concerning business drivers and forecasts. State all business, economic, and technical assumptions made in the production of the plan. This is quite difficult, since the most dangerous assumptions are those that we don't consciously make—witness the current difficulties in the Euro zone. You should be as rigorous as possible in stating the assumptions that underpin the stated plan and decisions.

Requested System Reserves

This section defines the reserve capacity of all system components required by the solution, including the following:

- Networking
- Servers
- Clients
- Applications

Component Capacity

This section identifies the solution's components (human, equipment, software, facilities, etc.) and defines the components' current capacities. You may record this information in a table that establishes the breakdown of the solution's various functional components and records relevant measurement parameters for the system's known capacity limits. Table A-3 establishes the breakdown of the various functional components of the system solution and records relevant measurement parameters for the known capacity limits for the system.

Table A-3. *Components and Their Known Capacity Limits*

Functional areas	Components	Configuration	Measurement	Capacity	Comments
Virtual Architecture					
Protocols and Transport					
Operating Systems					
Application Software					
Others					

Bottlenecks

This section describes any areas of the system solution that may represent functional bottlenecks.

Growth and Intervention Strategy

This section describes the manner in which the solution is envisioned to add additional capacity, such as the following:

- Incremental vs. replacement
- Horizontal vs. vertical scaling
- Parallel vs. hub spoke
- New technology

Service Summary

The service summary section should include the following subsections.

Current and Recent Service Provisions

For each service that is delivered, provide a service profile. This should include throughput rates and the resulting resource utilization (such as memory, storage space, transfer rates, processor usage, and network usage). Short-, medium-, and long-term trends should be presented here.

Service Forecasts

The business plans should provide capacity management with details of the new services planned and the growth or contraction in the use of existing services. This subsection should report on new services and the demise of legacy systems.

Findings Summary

If applicable, describe historical capacity growth patterns. Explain how future expected capacity requirements have been identified and analyzed. Outline recommendations for managing and addressing expected growth.

Insert a table/illustration, or provide a reference to where it is stored, that shows the different recommendations to address each of the capacity scenarios illustrated above. The example below will vary from project to project.

Describe how expected growth will be monitored and managed. Table A-4 is a basic example of a table that may be used to illustrate one approach for monitoring and managing future capacity. The approach used to illustrate these requirements may differ from project to project.

Table A-4. *Growth Predictions*

Area/Item Monitored	Capacity Requirement(s)	% Increase NeededPer (Time Period)	Capacity Threshold(s)	Threshold Response Strategy (Action to Be Take Upon Reaching Threshold(s))
< Server>	<Enter capacity requirements and measures>	<Enter projected increases over intervals of time>	<Enter acceptable capacity threshold(s)>	<Enter response strategies to varying threshold limits. *Threshold* is defined as the level at which an event or change occurs>

Resource Summary

This subsection concentrates on the resulting resource usage by the services. It reports, again, on the short-, medium-, and long-term trends in resource usage, broken down by hardware platform. This information has been gathered and analyzed by the subprocesses of service capacity management and component capacity management, and so should be readily available.

Options for Service Improvement

Building on the results of the previous section, this section outlines the possible options for improving the effectiveness and efficiency of service delivery. It could contain options for merging different services on a single processor, upgrading the network to take advantage of technological advances, tuning the use of resources or service performance, rewriting legacy systems, purchasing new hardware or software, etc.

Costs Forecast

The costs associated with these options should be documented here. In addition, the current and forecasted cost of providing IT services should be included. In practice, capacity management obtains much of this information from the financial management process and the IT financial plan.

Monitoring and Metrics

This section describes the various components that require monitoring for performance management. For example, a virtual server can be a component and its CPU utilization can be one of the metrics. This section describes the monitoring methods, techniques, and tools that will be used to evaluate solution and component performance, and provides metrics for planning intervention. This information should be provided for each major component at the solution level.

COMPONENT 1 <<SERVERS>>

COMPONENT 2 <<STORAGE>>

COMPONENT 3 <<COMPONENT>>

Thresholds for Intervention

This section identifies, describes, and quantifies thresholds for triggering intervention by changing component configuration.

Recommendations

The final section of the plan should contain a summary of the recommendations made in the previous plan and their status (for example, rejected, planned, implemented) and any variances from that plan. Any new recommendations in this iteration of the plan should be made here (i.e., which of the options mentioned in the plan is preferred). It should also include the implications if the plan, and its recommendations, are not implemented.

The recommendations should be quantified in terms of the following:

- Business benefits to be expected
- Potential impact of carrying out the recommendations
- Risks involved
- Resources required
- Costs, both set up and ongoing

Document History

This section specifies the latest version of the document and associated remarks as shown in Table A-5.

Table A-5. *The Document History Spreadsheet*

Date	Author	Version	Status	Description	Sections Affected

■ ■ ■

Capacity Implementation Case Study

Introduction and Scope

Now let's try to implement the concepts that you have learned through a case study and see how robust capacity planning processes help achieve cost reduction and adherence to SLAs.

For this case study, we will simplify things a little bit, cover the online e-commerce setup of a fictitious online retailer Myshop, and leave aside the other applications.

Myshop is a multinational retailer of technology, entertainment products, and services with a commitment to growth and innovation. The Myshop family of brands and partnerships collectively generates more than $2 billion in annual revenue. Myshop brands are available to customers through retail locations, call centers, and web sites, in-home solutions, product delivery, and community activities. These venues are backed by an aggressive expansion strategy across the globe. Presently, Myshop is interested in scenarios that will enable future growth, cloud adoption, IT infrastructure optimization, and reduced total cost of ownership (TCO). Myshop's IT infrastructure inventory includes approximately 2,000 end-user, network, and data center devices. Myshop's IT is running on 200 high-end servers.

Technology Vision

In conjunction with this business vision and expansion strategy, Myshop's IT infrastructure scalability adoption strategy is the key to its IT success. Capacity planning and management, together with cloud adoption, are the process areas that they expect will enable streamlined and responsive IT in order to achieve cost reduction and scalability. The two main goals are

- Leveraging new methods and breakthrough technologies
- Aligning IT with business and ensuring global expansion

Current Infrastructure Utilization and Cost Overview

With the increased scale of business operations and overall expansion strategy, there is an immediate requirement for IT scalability. Because of increased sales, branding, and marketing, the business is penetrating newer market segments and customers. Also, anticipated business demand inputs suggest the future capacity usage associated with the services offered. In addition, immediate attention is required to handle seasonal spikes that go up by 10 times normal usage.

In the next few years, Myshop is expecting the business to grow exponentially and this is backed by aggressive marketing and branding campaigns globally. IT must therefore plan and manage the business requirements utilizing optimum IT capacity. Business capacity requirements are determined on the following basis: Myshop's current server inventory is comprised of 200 servers, primarily Xeon 1270 quad core CPUs, 8 GB RAM, 750 SATA HDD, 3.2 GHz supporting more than 10,000 concurrent users at peak load. These servers are running in the hosting provider's data centers.

In an initial analysis, a key data point that came out was the server utilization rate. The current average server utilization rate was 55%, while the peak load utilization was around 95%, ensuring performance and uptime. However, with increased demand and the holiday season approaching, Myshop definitely needs to scale up the capacity to meet the increased demand. Myshop is faced with the choice of either buying capacity or moving to a cloud provider to scale out through a hybrid cloud approach that can meet the following challenges:

- Total capacity requirements must meet the current performance goals, future needs, and availability/recovery goals of all applications and services.

- Future proofing will be accomplished by having standby capacity ready in addition to what is currently being used.

- Availability/recovery is typically enabled through redundancy and data center tiers. This redundancy can be

  ✓ Component redundancy

  ✓ Full resource redundancy

  ✓ Data redundancy

- If demand exceeds capacity available for planned growth and/or does not leave enough redundant capacity, then it will compromise service levels.

- Either additional physical capacity will need to be added or workload will need to be removed from the pool of available capacity.

Figure B-1 describes the current and future IT capacity roadmap so that the business is served optimally.

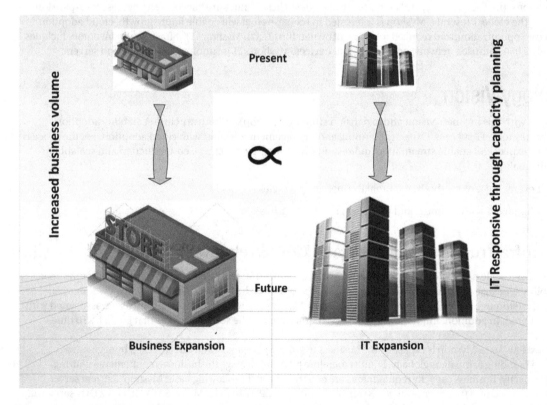

Figure B-1. *IT/business expansion*

IT Imperatives

Long-term IT imperatives include

- Cost effectiveness in IT expansion for meeting future business demand

- A clear understanding of the demands on services and future plans for workload growth or shrinkage

- Capacity planning in line with overall business objectives

- A commitment to meeting or exceeding agreed-upon SLAs

- Optimized infrastructure utilization rates

- Performance analysis of measurement data, including analysis of the impact of new services on current capacity

- Monitoring resources and system performance, system utilization, capacity limits, and expected capacity needs, and recording that information in the capacity management information system (CMIS).

- Performance tuning of activities to ensure the most efficient use of existing infrastructure

- A formal method for timely capacity projections to be included in Myshop's annual budget planning process

Need for Capacity Planning

The capacity planning activity ensures that the capacity of IT services and the IT infrastructure are able to deliver agreed service levels in a cost-effective manner. All resources must be considered to meet the demand forecast, which is based on the business requirements.

Myshop appreciates the role and importance of efficient capacity management processes for seamless business expansion. This ensures that increased capacity is implemented before capacity service level safety limits are breached. With this role in the enterprise, IT also seeks a transformation from a supplier to a service aggregator. As a service aggregator, IT serves the business with best of breed and cost-effective IT solutions. Thus, Myshop's IT transformation is the backbone of the overall IT strategy supporting the business.

This requires a review of capacity requirements as part of the normal business planning cycle and effective demand management.

All capacity-related requirements seek translation from business to service to component level (Figure B-2). Business-level requirements like increase in sales, seasonality, demand spikes, etc. need to be captured and the implications for service capacity need to be derived from them. Likewise, component capacity requirements need to be formulated and drafted.

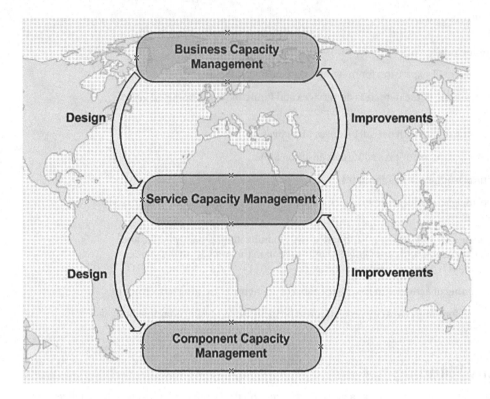

Figure B-2. *The now-familiar capacity management layers*

Implementing Capacity Management

The following subsections outline the steps to implement capacity management.

Step 1: Determine Capacity Requirements from Existing Monitoring Toolsets

Current performance monitoring tools and capacity reviews provide the information on current utilization and optimization requirements. These requirements are gathered from element monitoring tools through alarms, threshold reports, events, incidents, etc. Other toolsets that sit on top of basic monitoring systems provide meaningful information on capacity.

Capacity requirements for all new systems are fetched from existing toolsets in place to determine the necessary computer and network resources required, sizing such new systems, taking into account hardware utilization, requirements for resilience, performance of service levels, and cost.

After running discovery procedures in CMDB and analyzing them, the information snapshot in Table B-1 was taken on the current environment.

Table B-1. *Environment Snapshot*

Users	Servers	CPU Cores/Server	Avg. Utilization	Memory/Server
10000	200	4	55%	8

Capacity Demand Coupling

Demand management predicted the future needs, and this translation implied a 10% increase in servers yearly. This was done using pattern of business activities analysis and other demand management methods. Figure B-3 describes the relationship between capacity and demand. Demand helps in formulating future capacity requirements.

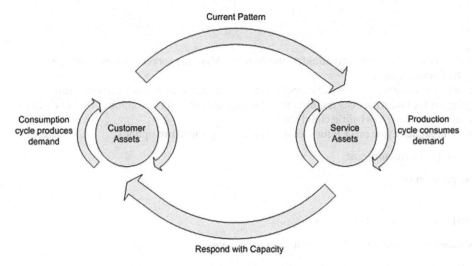

Demand Capacity Coupling

Figure B-3. *Demand/capacity coupling*

Demand analysis includes

- Demand during time of day/week/month/year

- Seasonal variations

- Special days (holiday season)

- Demand from different time zones

- Demand for different locations/data centers

Inputs for determining the number of users have been taken from the front end of Myshop's web portal. Myshop's current IT infrastructure on an average caters to 10,000 users at a time, managing a varied workload of users hitting the web portal, and maintaining response times.

Myshop's efficient demand management takes care of all future service forecasts. High seasonal variations during festivals have direct implications on Myshop's IT. To manage this demand, 200 servers are deployed in the server hosting model. During peak times, as mentioned earlier, server utilization goes up to 95% for a month. The rest of the year, server utilization range is 45-55%. On average, there is a 10% increase in server inventory year on year to meet regular yearly increases in demand.

Myshop is expecting the following demand scenario:

- ✓ Holiday season for 1 month : 10x the users on the web site

- ✓ Yearly growth of traffic on the web site: 10% year on year growth

These figures were arrived at using demand management and a robust capacity management process along with implementation of tools and data analysis.

Therefore, the following was concluded:

- ✓ Compute capacity needed for 1 peak month: 2000 servers (x10 times)
- ✓ Compute capacity increase in year 1: 20 servers (10% increase)
- ✓ Compute capacity increase in year 2: 22 servers (10% increase)

Cost of Capacity

Now, in order to maintain the performance and accommodate the demand, Myshop's server inventory required 10x capacity during the high demand season.

Financial budgets drive IT spending on increases in capacity. Financial budgets in conjunction with future demands are determining factors for future capacity requirements. Myshop is evaluating the options of either opting for a dedicated infrastructure or switching to a hybrid cloud model.

Myshop must compute the capacity year on year for increased costs using one of two options.

> Option 1: Dedicated infrastructure cost
>
> Option 2: Cloud provider cost

Option 1: Dedicated Infrastructure

The cost incurred in a dedicated infrastructure includes the following elements:

- ✓ Data center space
- ✓ Power
- ✓ Rack
- ✓ Compute
- ✓ Network
- ✓ Bandwidth
- ✓ Storage
- ✓ Set up
- ✓ Maintenance and management

The above-mentioned environment includes running 1800 servers with varying utilization rates as mentioned earlier to accommodate demand. Servers with configuration Xeon 1270 quad core, 8GB RAM, 750 SATA HDD, 3.2 GHz processors from a hosting provider currently comes to **$13,000,000** yearly for 1,800 servers. Additional cost elements incurred include management, monitoring, maintenance costs, etc.

Option 2: Cloud Provider

In the cloud provider proposed hybrid cloud model, for peak months, the additional server requirements of 1800 are fulfilled from a public cloud (i.e., AWS).

In this scenario, as shown in the Figure B-4, Myshop is considering the use of 200 existing servers and an additional 1,800 from a public cloud, and the cost is shown in Table B-2.

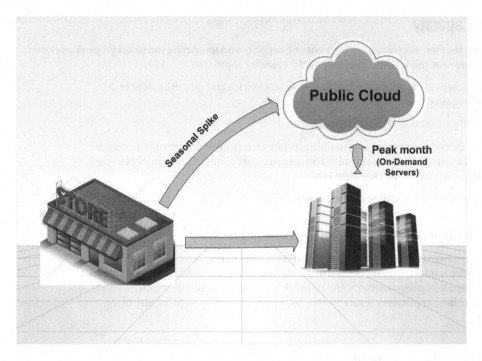

Figure B-4. *Scalability during peak*

Table B-2. *Environment Snapshot*

Users	Servers	CPU/User	Utilization	Memory/Server	Cloud cost $
90000	1800	4	95%	8	**4,000,000**

Now, including cloud management, monitoring, high availability, 99.9 SLAs, and other automations, the total cost of cloud-based servers turned out to be $4,000,000.

The outcome of this cost analysis is fed to the financial management process for setting the yearly budget, and based on financial feasibility, planning and budgeting, funds are allocated to the best solution.

Performance Targets

The performance targets are the targets set through automated testing and service level monitoring tools. These tools automatically gather performance related requirements to set new thresholds dynamically. This helps in establishing new performance benchmarks and SLAs. These tools help in specifying measures and requirements in terms of response time and other performance related measures.

Step 2: Design for Capacity

The hybrid cloud approach resulted in utilization of the existing capacity and leveraging the cloud for peak workloads. The following considerations were made while establishing the capacity approach:

- ✓ Removal of fragmented capacity may lead to high inefficiencies and may even double the infrastructure required to host the workloads.

- ✓ To ensure intelligent allocation of virtual machines.

- ✓ To consider toolsets that are capable of defining technical, business, and compliance rules for workload placement. These workload placement rules are configured in cloud lifecycle management toolsets in the management layer.

- ✓ Rule engines are used to guarantee the health and accuracy of the capacity management solution.

- ✓ Following architecture principles that are resilient, agile, and scalable.

- ✓ Capacity management is able to establish application related needs like multi-tenancy, associated service level requirements, infrastructure requirements, scalability requirements, disk space, compute capacity, memory and network bandwidth requirements, etc. These measures help in planning future system requirements and the architecture of the environment.

Establish the Capacity Architecture

The following are the considerations for establishing MyShop's capacity architecture. These architecture guidelines are primarily considered to meet MyShop's dynamic business needs.

- ✓ Scalability of an application allows it to be scaled out to accommodate the growth. Layered-based architecture for capacity management should be established with a defined set of protocols between the various layers. At the bottom of this layered architecture is the virtualization layer. This can either be a server, network, or storage virtualization layer.

- ✓ Tools are used to monitor the virtualization layer and underlying virtual clusters, farms, and machines including servers, network, and storage.

- ✓ At this layer, virtual machine profiling can be done, which assists in trending procedures. This is the elementary layer and demand data, in terms of usage and utilization rate, and is fetched from the virtual environment.

- ✓ Usage details like CPU, memory, disk space, disk I/O bandwidth, and network I/O bandwidth are taken into account by the usage analysis layer that sits on top of the monitoring layer.

- ✓ Future trends of capacity are calculated based on statistical analysis.

- ✓ At this layer, the capacity model forecasts the behavior of infrastructure using demand, financial, operational, application performance, and vendor-related data. Application sizing estimates the resource requirements to support the application to ensure that the SLAs are met. Application sizing also helps in identifying resource consumption and cost implications for new or changed applications and their effect on other related applications.

Apply Capacity Techniques

These techniques can be used to model and optimize the capacity design.

- ✓ Most of the capacity techniques are based on scientific methods and application of predictive modeling technology powered by proven queuing theory algorithms.

- ✓ Simulation of virtualization activities must be performed to identify the best candidates, targets, and optimal placements (for example, according to compatible workloads) with respect to technical, geographical, business, and compliance criteria.

- ✓ A simulation is able to depict how a service scales from a test environment to a production-level environment by using load testing results.

- ✓ A simulation of infrastructure changes (for example, horizontal or vertical scaling or failover) and business change scenarios is conducted (for example, business trends and marketing plans.)

Step 3: Produce Capacity Plan

The capacity plan, based on existing and future business demand, is developed and distributed. This includes information on

- SLAs
- Application specifications
- Current infrastructure
- User task scenarios
- Task load matrices
- Monitoring and metrics
- Forecasts
- Service tiers, etc.

Step 4: Ongoing Capacity Management

During operations, data (like server utilization, etc.) is fetched from various underlying tools and associated data sources. This data provides capacity management with process health reports and other key performance indicators. These information sources can then be used to provide a unified reporting portal to assist in capacity monitoring and planning for the cloud, service, and underlying components.

The current capacity solution is also for end-to-end monitoring and analysis of virtualized environments. The monitoring and analysis of infrastructure usage by customers are two prime areas of iterative capacity management, followed by tuning and implementation. This is an ongoing capacity optimization cycle.

Actual Ongoing Capacity Management Tool

The cloud provider implemented VMware vCenter operations management suite based on capacity best practices for ongoing operations and capacity management. As shown in Figure B-5, this tool ensures all ongoing capacity management activities are performed efficiently. Now, with the right set of analytical and forecasting toolsets in place, ongoing capacity management is comprised of four prime optimization activities.

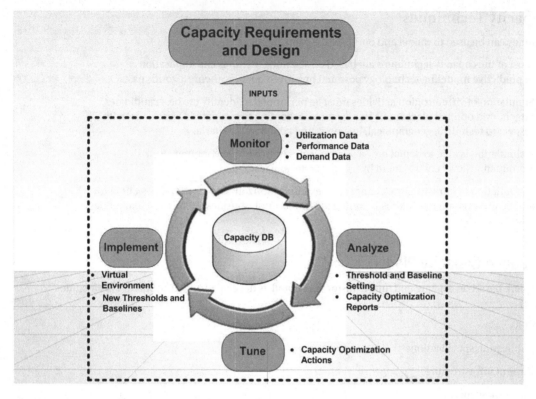

Figure B-5. *Ongoing capacity management framework*

- **Implementation:** Implementing capacity and supporting virtualization management techniques like DRS, clustering, memory ballooning, scaling, etc.

- **Monitoring:** Monitoring utilization and performance

- **Analysis:** Analyzing capacity data for trending and forecasting

- **Tuning:** Optimization actions for improved resource utilization and performance

These activities provide the basic historical information and triggers necessary for all of the other activities and processes within capacity management. Monitors are established on all the components and for each of the services.

The data is analyzed using expert systems to compare usage levels against thresholds wherever possible. The results of the analysis are included in reports, and recommendations are made as appropriate.

Control mechanisms are in place to act on the recommendations. This may take the form of balancing services, balancing workloads, changing concurrency levels, and adding or removing resources.

All of the information accumulated during these activities is stored in the capacity management database and the cycle (implement, monitor, analyze, tuning) then begins again, monitoring any changes made to ensure they have had a beneficial effect and collecting more data for future actions.

The cloud solution provider implemented a VMware platform for the virtualization and capacity management suite supporting the following features for efficient and effective environment management, optimization, tracking, resource utilization, workload movement, etc.:

- Scaling

- Clustering

- Load balancing

- Memory ballooning

- Swapping

- Distributed resource scheduling

- Cloud orchestration

- Hybrid cloud management

For ongoing monitoring, analysis, and tuning, the vCenter Operations Manager gathers, analyzes, and presents all performance and monitoring-related requirements. This is shown in Figure B-6. This ensures automated operations and management use of analytics and an integrated approach to performance, capacity, and configuration management. The VMware solution provides effective management, control, and visibility over Myshop's cloud environment, enabling better actionable intelligence proactively.

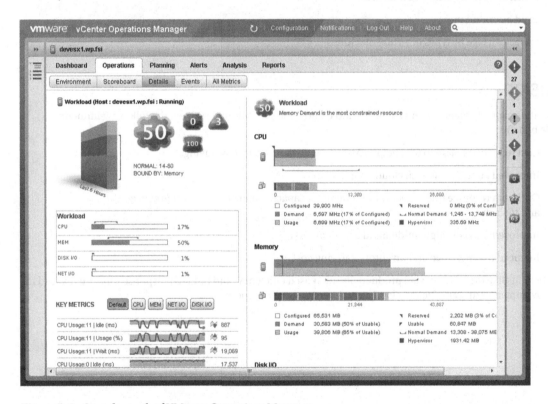

Figure B-6. *Sample graph of VMware Operations Manager*

Step 5: Capacity Review

All capacity reports in CDB are exported to other process areas in customized formats and views. On the basis of consolidated reporting and an updated capacity database, strategic decision making is supported. Reports include

- ✓ Overall capacity available

- ✓ Overall capacity used

- ✓ Overall capacity unused

- ✓ Forecast report for cloud capacity available/used

- ✓ Forecast for demand

- ✓ Data center/location reports

- ✓ Underutilized/overutilized forecasts

- ✓ Yield per cloud unit

- ✓ Capacity usage by types of virtual machines

Conclusion

By implementing capacity management solutions and cloud adoption, Myshop realized the following immediate, quantifiable benefits:

- Cost reductions of up to 65% helped Myshop with substantial cost savings

- Improved IT agility through cloud enablement

- Optimum resource utilization by implementing capacity management best practices and toolsets

- Improved SLAs through on-demand access of service

- Reduced maintenance and inventory carrying cost

Other benefits like increases in staff productivity, increased efficiency, and reduced response time are realized in due course by implementing an efficient cloud capacity management process.

Index